I0111318

IT'S NOT MAGIC; IT'S FREQUENCY

SHIFT YOUR ENERGY AND SHAPE YOUR RESULTS

CAROLINA CHAMS

AMA PUBLISHING

CONTENTS

To you, Mami.

My number one fan.

The one who has always believed in me, even in the moments when I doubted myself.

Thank you for holding me up with your unconditional love, for taking care of my children when I needed to take care of my soul… and also when I needed to chase my dreams.

Thank you for being there, for supporting, for lifting me with faith, presence, and even sponsorships, every step of the way. You have been the light in my darkest days and the fuel on my longest journeys.

Your faith in me has been one of the greatest gifts of my life.

This book is also yours.

Because without you, many of my dreams would never have taken off.

I love you with all my heart.

Thank you for giving me life… and for teaching me to live it with love.

FOREWORD
SOME BOOKS TEACH. OTHERS AWAKEN.

It's Not Magic; it's Frequency —*does both-and then it lovingly invites you into something even deeper: alignment with your truest, most radiant self.*

*When my dear friend Caro first shared the **5 R's** with me — **Recognize, Reset, Redirect, Rebuild, and Reclaim** — I didn't just hear them. **I felt them.***

It was an experience that lifted me from challenge into clarity, from heaviness into hope, uncertainty to confirmation. These weren't just catchy concepts-they were life-giving, spirit-anchoring truths that, when practiced with intention, create the kind of inner shift that leads to outer transformation.

During a difficult season of my life, Caro walked me through each of those Rs over the phone -and in a matter of minutes, everything began to change.

My energy lifted. My thoughts cleared. My path realigned. And suddenly, what once felt impossible began unfolding with ease.

That's the power of frequency. That's the beauty of co-creating with God.

This book isn't about hustling your way into a new version of yourself or the cliched "follow these steps" recipe for life. It's about coming home to the one you've always been. It's about clearing space-not by force, but through love-for the life that's been quietly waiting for you. It's about remembering who you are, releasing who you're not, and making room for your sacred spirit to rise.

*And while this isn't a religious book, make no mistake-**there is divine grace all over it**.*

Walking in this frequency draws you closer to something greater. It creates room for a deeper connection with God, one that feels natural, gentle, and real.

If you already have that relationship, it will deepen.

If you don't, you may just discover it here-in the quiet shifts, in the healing pauses, in the moments where your heart finally exhales...

And then... there's my Carito, as I like to call her.

Oh, how I adore this woman.

She is my soul sister, my accountability partner, my mastermind co-pilot, and yes-my unofficial therapist. (Compensation? Tight hugs, voice notes, and lots of funny GIFs.)

*One of my favorite memories with her was the day she introduced us-me and our mastermind sisters-to her signature somatic energy release technique, brilliantly (and very accurately) named **Saca Saca** which in Spanish means "get it out."*

And baby, we got it ALL out. We were shaking, shimmying, kicking, and laughing so hard. It was part dance party, part therapy session, and 100% pure, untamed freedom.

I'm convinced these moves deserve to go viral.

TikTok ain't ready for the Saca Saca-but the world needs it!

It deserves a book of its own.

And lucky for you, you'll get a taste of it in the chapters ahead.

It's simple. It's powerful. It's unforgettable. And once you experience it, you'll want to do it again and again.

Caro doesn't just teach frequency, she is frequency. She lives what she speaks with grace, soul, humor, and so much heart. Get excited! If this book found its way into your hands, I believe it's because you're ready

Ready for more peace.

More clarity.

More **you**.

And I promise, you're in the best hands.

So take a deep breath. Be open. Give yourself grace.

Let these words rise up to meet you like a cool breeze on a warm day.

This isn't magic-it's remembering. *And it's your time.*

With all my love and belief in you,

Eliza M. Garza

Best-Selling Award-Winning Author

INTRODUCTION

And what if I told you that you're not stuck, but disconnected from your true frequency?

I'm sitting on the rooftop of **Casa Limón**, closing this chapter of my life in this hidden gem: a stone-built house surrounded by vibrant flowers and the lush vegetation of Guanajuato, in La Presita, just a few kilometers from the enchanting *pueblo mágico* (Magic Town) of San Miguel de Allende. Until less than a month ago, I had no idea where I'd end up writing this story.

I clearly remember the trip I took to San Miguel about seven years ago with my childhood friends from Barranquilla. We stayed in a cozy hotel in the heart of the city, where the bells of the Church of San Miguel Arcángel woke us each morning as a reminder that we hadn't come to rest, but to celebrate our friendship, explore every nook of the town, and enjoy a few days of freedom, away from husbands and children. It was an unforgettable trip, full of laughter, anecdotes, and memories I still treasure.

But this visit has been different.

This time, I came alone.

Without the bustle of friends or family, without restaurant reservations or shopping plans. I came with only one purpose: **to write.**

I met Christina Limón at a Latina Empire retreat in South Padre Island, Texas, where I was one of the hosting coaches and leaders. She attended as a guest of my dear Nigerian friend, Esther Akindayomi. We were a group of forty women in search of healing and transformation. At the end of the retreat, Christina approached me to ask if my "oracle of universe messages" was available in English. I told her it was in Spanish but that I had a PDF with the translation and I'd gladly send it. In that brief conversation, she mentioned she used to visit San Miguel and was building a house there. We hadn't seen each other since—until recently, during another talk I led, where we barely exchanged a distant greeting.

A few hours before that talk, I made a conscious decision: I needed to travel for a week to finish my book. At home, I couldn't flow amid chores, family routine, and mental noise. My heart whispered: **San Miguel is the place.** It was my first choice. A completely intuitive decision.

San Miguel de Allende has been a refuge for artists, writers, and creative souls for generations. It wouldn't surprise me if Gabriel García Márquez, during his time in Mexico, was inspired by this very place. That idea resonated in me. Just imagining that I'd write my work here completely elevated my frequency.

While driving to the event, I called my mom and asked if she could take care of the kids. She, my number-one fan—the one who believes in me most on the face of the Earth—agreed without a second thought. Still, she recommended I check the costs, especially lodging, because to her, it sounded more like a luxury getaway than a spiritual mission. But I decided not to let those details lower my vibrational frequency.

—*"I'll figure it out,"* I told her, with the certainty that comes from the soul when it has decided.

That night, it wasn't by chance that my talk was titled **"Energy Matters: The Art of Elevating Your frequency."** The energy was at its peak. I radiated my best self to that beautiful, powerful audience. The atmosphere was soaked in gratitude, sisterhood, delicious tacos, and the bright spark of so many inspiring women gathered.

When I arrived home that night, I asked my subconscious for a clear sign. I needed to sort out the trip as soon as possible to deliver my manuscript on time. I'm used to giving my subconscious work before sleep since it holds 95% of our beliefs, traumas, habits, and never rests. The subconscious works 24 hours a day, so you must put it to work on productive things, not mental garbage.

The next morning, upon opening my eyes, I remembered: **Christina!** She had mentioned her house in San Miguel. I wrote to her immediately:

"Hi Christina, it was great seeing you yesterday at the event. Hey, were you the one who said you have a house in San Miguel? I'm writing a book and want to be inspired in a place like that. Do you have any recommendations?"

Her reply was almost immediate:

"Yes, indeed I have a house there. You can go whenever you want… at no cost."

At no cost!

What happened next was one of those moments of pure manifestation. One of those where everything aligns with divine precision. In less than 24 hours, the universe responded. The universe spoke loud and clear. Everything aligned with divine perfection.

And I understood: this book had to speak about those quantum leaps we take when we stop controlling, when we open ourselves to receive from faith and pure intention.

My heart overflowed with emotion and gratitude. I was surprised— and yet not—that someone I barely knew would offer me her sanctuary without asking anything in return. But I felt it deeply: **these things happen to me.** And they no longer astonish me.

I deserve them. I attract them effortlessly. I am abundant. I am prosperous. I receive in the same measure that I give.

I accepted her generous invitation with a glowing soul, and in the blink of an eye, the trip was already underway. Everything flowed. My heart was ready to write, and the universe, once again, gave me the perfect nudge.

It was seven days. And just as God created the world in seven days, I wrote this book in that same span.

It wasn't coincidence. It was a download. An act of surrender and absolute presence.

What for many might seem an impossible feat, for me was the exact and divinely assigned time.

It wasn't pressure, it was inspiration.

It wasn't effort, it was alignment.

When you focus your mind with clarity, intention, and a burning desire, something activates: infinite intelligence sets into motion and begins orchestrating everything in your favor. There is no logic. There's no human calendar that can explain it. There's only connection. Because when you're truly connected, time stops being an obstacle and becomes your ally.

It stretches, adjusts, opens. **It transforms.**

Time, as we conceive it, is an illusion. And in those seven days I confirmed it. I was so present, so surrendered, so synchronized with the Source, that the words didn't write... **they poured.** Each day was a portal, each silence a prayer, each page an answer. The clock didn't mark hours, **it marked frequencies.**

And so I understood that when you align, time becomes sacred space.

In that space, creation happens frictionlessly, without anguish, without resistance.

It happens from the soul.

And when something is born from the soul, it isn't measured by how long it takes, **but by how much it transforms.**

Each day at Casa Limón was a revelation.

From the golden light that bathed the rooftop at dawn to the starry nights that whispered words. Every moment was a portal toward my creativity, a sacred space where everything flowed with purpose.

Writing this book made me realize that I'm not just sharing knowledge and experiences. I'm sharing my story, yes… but more than that, **I'm extending an invitation to you.**

A real, loving, spacious invitation for you to also allow yourself to dream big, elevate your frequency, and remember the creative power that lives in you.

Each story holds a lesson, a tool, a key to help transform your reality. Throughout these pages you'll also find messages I received during my own healing process—channelings, intuitions, phrases planted in the silence—and that I share today with you to accompany you in yours.

You can feel the magic… because **magic is that energy that transforms the impossible into possible.**

Not the one we were taught in stories or the one hidden behind tricks and wands.

I believe in real, tangible, creative magic… **the kind that's born from within.**

That magic that activates when you elevate your frequency, when you align with your truth, when you trust the process, and choose to manifest from the soul.

It's not external magic. It's not luck. It's not coincidence.

It's frequency.

And when you vibrate high, you create miracles.

You don't need to exhaust yourself or fight against the world to achieve your goals.

The path of constant sacrifice isn't the only one. Another exists: that of aligned energy, focused intention, and deep connection with your purpose.

When you activate your highest frequency, opportunities begin to find you.

The right people arrive. The doors open.

Resources flow to you without needing to chase them.

And everything begins to feel lighter, more natural, more true.

My intention isn't to teach you something new, but to help you remember what already lives in you.

To awaken that wise, intuitive, magnetic part that's been buried under the noise of the world or the wounds of the past.

If you're reading this, it's no coincidence.

Something inside you is ready to **elevate its frequency.**

This book is a compass to reconnect you with your essence, take energetic control of your life, and manifest from certainty.

Because you don't need to have everything figured out to begin. You just need to take the first step... and trust.

Trust that the universe conspires in your favor.

Trust that your energy creates your reality.

Because:

"Opportunities aren't sought. They're created from your frequency."

Welcome to this journey.

The magic in your life is remembering who you are... and how you vibrate.

CHAPTER ONE
THE HOLLOW

"How do I get out of this hole?"

That was the question echoing loudest in my mind when, just one week after arriving in the United States with my three small children, I was served with divorce papers.

It had been a brave leap into the unknown: moving into a borrowed house owned by my in-laws, which was vacant at the time, in a city I hadn't chosen—trusting that everything would work out. The plan seemed logical: take advantage of the border proximity to process my residency after ten years of marriage. The idea was simple and promising: I would get my green card, the kids would learn English, and in one year, everything would return to normal.

Just one year? How hard could it be?

I remember a Woody Allen quote that said:

"If you want to make God laugh, tell Him your plans."

In that moment, that phrase made more sense than ever, because my plans now felt broken, undone. What was supposed to be a year of adjustment was turning, suddenly, into the uncertainty of an undesired stay.

And why go back to Mexico? The only reason I had moved to Ciudad del Carmen—a petroleum island I had grown to love but knew deep down would never be my forever home—was that marriage, which was now crumbling.

But reality hit me hard. I was in McAllen—without family, without a job, without my own home, and worst of all, without any affection for the place. I had a roof, yes, but it was definitely not the place I could imagine rebuilding my life. I looked toward Miami, but with three kids in tow? I wasn't sure. Austin had my grandma and aunts, but the same question persisted: **how was I going to support all of this?**

Returning to Barranquilla wasn't even on the table.

The truth was, I had no idea what was going to happen or how I was going to survive. I felt stranded in a thick, dark limbo.

Then, amidst that internal storm, a voice emerged in my mind—soft but firm:

"The How isn't your problem; I'll take care of it."

Was that you, God? That thought surprised me. It didn't seem to come from me—if it were mine, it wouldn't have carried such deep, immediate peace. Maybe it wasn't God, maybe it was an angel... or even my dad, speaking from somewhere in heaven. Whoever it was, I was sure of one thing: **it didn't come from this earthly realm.**

And if it gave me calm in the middle of chaos, it had to be a message of light.

I decided to listen.

I decided to believe it.

But it wasn't easy.

Every time I tried to move forward, resistance returned.

Sometimes stronger than before.

Just thinking about the future wrenched my soul and body, as if the air became denser, heavier, almost impossible to breathe.

There I was, stuck in a deep hole, wondering if there really was a way out.

The hole felt ever darker, and with it came resentments.

Resentments toward myself, my partner, and life itself, for delivering me this sudden turn.

Guilt tightened my chest:

Didn't I want a divorce… or did I?

Doubts danced in my head like relentless ghosts, unraveling everything inside.

Reality became overwhelming; facing all this without help, without family nearby, was like sailing in a stormy sea.

I couldn't afford to collapse or cry openly, because my three little ones were by my side, looking at me with those innocent eyes.

They didn't yet understand what separation meant, but they felt the fear of facing the unknown: a new school, new friends, a completely different life. They only thought about surviving that first day of classes without knowing English.

Though inside I felt shattered, I decided to face my grief without masks.

I showed strength when necessary, but I also allowed myself to be vulnerable.

I did the best I could with what I had.

My days were filled with such deep pain that the darkness I was in seemed endless.

Everything I did, every step I took, was wrapped in such low energy that it kept me trapped in that abyss with no exit.

Getting out of bed felt like a heroic act.

I just wanted to sleep… and not wake up.

It felt like being buried under wet sand or carrying a sack of cement: any attempt to climb out left me exhausted before I even started.

The house was full of photos of his family.

Images representing a family that was no longer mine, but was still there, witnesses to a love that was fading.

Walking those halls felt like carrying bags of sand full of memories, silent reproaches, and unprocessed emotions.

Each step pulled me deeper into the hole I was trying to escape.

Cleaning the house—a task that was always an effort—now was triple the effort.

I felt every rag was heavier, the broom uncooperative, the floor never clean enough.

But it wasn't just the external mess weighing me down…

It was internal chaos.

The emotional turmoil that followed me into every corner.

Dropping the kids off at school also made me feel guilty.

I felt a sort of relief—a small breath… and that same feeling made me feel worse.

But I saw them so brave, facing this new stage with a mix of nerves and curiosity, that all I could do was admire them.

Yet, it hurt me deeply to leave them in a place I also felt was unknown.

I couldn't be there to protect them. And that broke me inside.

In that sea of emotions, my energy continued to sink.

And the hole… felt ever darker, ever deeper.

As if with every step I moved further from the light.

And then there was the kitchen—always a space that indifferently stirred me.

In Mexico and Colombia, I'd always relied on help to manage it—a normalized luxury in our culture. Having a housekeeper to cook or clean was part of my routine, freeing me to focus elsewhere without guilt.

But now, in this new home, the kitchen became a mirror of my vulnerability.

A responsibility I could no longer delegate.

No support, no energy, no desire.

Instead of a space of nourishment and creativity, it became a battlefield where every dirty dish towered like an impossible mountain to climb.

What was I going to cook? With what spirit?

I didn't even enjoy it.

And in those moments, I felt so incapable of everything that even frying an egg felt like an achievement.

But amid all this pain, I knew I had to find a way to cope—not just for me, but for them.

I had to find a path, even if that path was full of uncertainty and fear.

So I decided to create a sacred space, a kind of personal sanctuary where I could shelter from the chaos.

I opened the door to a bedroom and began emptying the place—removing furniture and the mattress I no longer needed.

This would be my refuge, **my meditation room.**

With determination, I told myself:

"I'm going to start meditating again, hoping to receive divine illumination—from my higher self, from my angels, ancestors, and guides."

I was done being trapped in darkness.

"Come on, Carolina! You've never given up. It's time to take inspired action."

And so I left the house, with new energy bubbling inside me, ready to be transformed.

I headed to the bookstore, where I bought every self-help and personal development book that caught my attention.

Each title was a beacon—a promise of new beginnings and possibilities.

I returned with my treasures:

- Essential oils to ground and reconnect me
- Sage to cleanse the stagnant energy
- Palo santo to seal in the renewed frequency
- Crystals with powerful intention: black tourmaline for protection, amethyst for mental and spiritual clarity, rose quartz for self-love
- Notebooks to resume writing and journaling
- Candles to create an atmosphere of light and intention

And of course, after so much internal chaos, I finally did what my soul had been asking all along:

I sought guidance.

I called the mentors and friends who had accompanied different chapters of my life:

the astrologer, the Kabbalist, the divorce coach, the angelologist.

I contacted the tarot reader and the psychologist.

I went to church.

I was willing to enlighten myself with every conversation, every tool, every glimmer of wisdom that would light another candle inside me.

In that new sanctuary, surrounded by light and renewed energy, I sat to meditate.

As I breathed deeply, I felt each inhale fill me with possibility, and each exhale release the weight that had bound me for too long.

With each passing day, I began to discover the strength inside me.

And little by little, the dark hole began to lighten.

CHAPTER TWO

THE 99%

In the meditation room, I began to remember who I was in essence.

That strong, reliable, unconditional woman who faced challenges with courage and didn't believe in the impossible.

The one who felt deeply, loved intensely, and dreamed big.

My tears —a mix of pain, gratitude, and hope— intertwined like an emotional rainbow illuminating my being.

It was then that I heard a *female voice* softly say:

"Hello."

I was alone at home, and that voice rang so clearly it gave me chills.

I didn't feel fear.

I made sure there was no one else, and when I confirmed it, I had no doubt that this voice came from the **99%**.

When I explored the wisdom of Kabbalah, I understood that the **1%** represents the physical plane: what we see, touch, smell, taste, and hear.

But the **99%** is the spiritual realm, where angels, guides, masters, and the pure energy of the Creator reside.

Accessing that plane is a divine advantage: it's connecting with what's essential.

Was it the Virgin Mary?

I had a sculpture of her in my room.

Or maybe my grandmother?

Or Meira Delmar, my great-aunt poet?

Or an angel?

I felt a mix of curiosity and reverence.

"What do you want to tell me? Speak more!" I whispered.

But there were no more words.

Only the certainty that something was waiting for me in the spiritual world.

I decided to search for that information.

It became my new life purpose.

While taking care of my children and healing my wounds, I began a path toward the invisible, with the intention of reconnecting with my essence.

I started researching angels and discovered that they communicate in clear, creative, and loving ways, using symbols we can easily recognize.

I asked for a sign.

I spoke to them with my heart:

"Angels, if you can hear me, I want my sign to communicate with you to be a white feather."

Even though I knew it was a common sign, I had never seen a feather appear out of nowhere.

But this time, I decided **to believe.**

I needed to.

One day, I took my kids to Anita and Robe's house, Marilía's parents —my soul sister and the only person I knew in McAllen.

Our friendship had started in college and had grown stronger during the hardest moments of my life.

The day my father passed away, I happened to be in Miami, staying at Marilía's house.

With her, I experienced my first grief… and also the second.

It was no coincidence that it was her who awaited me in this unfamiliar city.

Marilía has undoubtedly been a soul mate on this plane.

What were the chances that, among so many people in the world, she would be the only one I knew in McAllen just when I needed someone the most?

Behind all of it was a divine gift, perfectly orchestrated.

While the kids played in the private community pool, I was reading a book about angels and followed the book's advice: **ask for a clear sign.**

The white feather.

I felt a deep certainty.

As if my energy had passed through a portal.

Only a few minutes passed.

Suddenly, I saw something floating toward me.

At first, I thought it was a leaf, but as I got closer I realized:

it was a white feather, perfect.

I picked it up gently, as if I were holding a miracle in my hands.

The tears flowed on their own.

In that moment, I knew I wasn't alone.

The 99% exists. And it communicates clearly.

"Oh, Father God, what else do you have for me?" I thought, with a smile that bloomed from the depths of my soul.

I felt I had started a new relationship with the spiritual world.

I had my sign.

I had my bridge.

I didn't know how my angels or guides would reveal themselves, but I understood something vital:

the how wasn't my problem.

The months that followed were so impactful that I began to record each sign.

The white feathers kept appearing… but now my "little guys" (as I started calling my angels) got creative.

One morning, after dropping my kids off at school, I opened the front door.

I don't remember if I was getting the mail or simply going out for air.

What I'll never forget is what I found:

another white feather, on the doormat, in a roofed and enclosed space.

It didn't make sense… but there it was.

I smiled.

"Thank you," I whispered, though inside I still hurt.

I felt stuck, lost.

"Thank you for the feather, but I'm still sad… what do I do now? Am I on the right path?" I asked.

A few days later, I went out to the garden.

And what I saw left me speechless: **dozens, maybe hundreds of tiny white feathers** were scattered all over the lawn.

I searched for a logical explanation: a bird attacked? a fight between animals?

But there were no signs of anything —just those immaculate feathers.

I felt an inner voice telling me:

"You are not alone. You have a legion of angels with you. The mind doubts, but you choose what to believe."

And I chose to believe.

I chose to trust in what can't be seen but can be felt.

I walked into the house with feathers in hand and kept many of them in a glass jar.

That jar became a tangible reminder of the invisible.

Over time, the feathers kept appearing… and still do.

Some I find in my car, others in unexpected places.

I remember one in particular: I was having lunch with my cousin Vicky in a restaurant in South Beach, and while we were talking about my dad, **a feather fell right in front of me.**

We looked at each other in silence, stunned, speechless.

Our skin bristled and we began to laugh.

It was one of those moments where time seemed to stop.

She, with wide eyes, said to me:

"Did you see that?"

And I could only smile with teary eyes and say:

"It's my dad."

I felt such deep peace flooding my whole body.

It was as if that feather had its own voice, as if it were silently saying:

"You are not alone. You never have been."

Every time a feather appears, I smile.

Because I know I'm on the right path.

Because I know they accompany me, care for me, and guide me.

And this relationship with the spiritual world is not exclusive.

You can have it too.

We all come from the same source.

We all have access to that loving guidance.

Sometimes, that guidance speaks to you in the language you understand:

through repeating numbers, butterflies, hummingbirds, songs, scents, books, social media posts, or even phrases in a TV series.

Because God and the universe —or whatever you want to call it— always find a way to speak to you when you're willing to listen.

So if you ever feel lost or disconnected, remember:

help is always closer than you think.

You just have to ask for it.

Open yourself to the invisible.

Allow the little miracles to find you.

You choose the sign.

And when it comes, it will remind you of what your soul already knows:

The 99% is real.

It's available.

And it wants to guide you.

CHAPTER THREE

THE BLESSED DARKNESS

My divorce was anything but simple.

It was chaotic and draining, like navigating turbulent waters without knowing how to sail a boat, without a captain, and with a vulnerable crew barely staying afloat.

There was geographical separation, a change of residence, language, schools, work... not to mention the gossip, rumors, lies, and threats that came and went amid the emotional chaos of all the parties involved. All of it stirred up deep wounds that began to surface like protective shields to avoid further suffering.

I firmly believe that there are levels to divorce. While I'm convinced that none are easy for anyone, there are nuances that make a difference. The real gap between a devastating experience and a more manageable one lies in how you handle that emotional rollercoaster, how you respond to low blows, how you communicate to your children what's happening and, above all, how you protect your peace and mental health.

The key lies in letting go of resistance and learning to quiet the ego. But even more importantly, it's about not giving away your power or control to people or external circumstances when you're most vulnerable. You must remember the potential you carry within —the power of your own mind— to avoid being consumed by misfortune. Because in a divorce, personal damage and collateral effects on children, family members, and even businesses are often inevitable.

For me, it was the first time I had faced such a raw and painful situation. To this day, I consider it the hardest experience of my life. Even more than the death of my father, which at 20 years old plunged me into an abyss I didn't climb out of for years. I lost myself in drugs and alcohol, making countless mistakes that could have easily cost me my life.

However, the divorce marked the breaking point that allowed me to confirm the core premise of this book: that it's possible to transform your energy into opportunities and emerge from stagnation not only standing, but stronger, clearer, and deeply connected to yourself.

It wasn't easy, but it was profound. And most of all, real.

With the help of my inner power —and my magic wand: gratitude— I began to rebuild myself step by step. Like a phoenix rising from its own ashes, my process was painful but also liberating. And although the pain could have crushed me, I chose to turn it into fuel to lift me higher.

I had to learn to look at my ex-husband soul to soul, not ego to ego. It took me years to change my perception and recognize him as the hero of this story. I became convinced that this had already been agreed upon before birth, or in past lives, and that he was simply fulfilling his part of the contract. And that somehow, discovering this would bring a reward.

While I waited for that reward, the universe kept testing me.

And that's why it had to rain on already soaked ground —or so I thought— when, in the middle of the divorce chaos, the universe decided to top it off with something unexpected: **the pandemic.**

"If you don't come to Pengilly right now, you're going to be stuck in McAllen, broke, without help, and going crazy alone with three kids."

Those were my mother's exact words when everything shut down due to COVID-19 and the world fell into uncertainty.

She and my stepfather lived in a small town in Minnesota, with barely 270 inhabitants, houses scattered around a serene lake surrounded by pine trees, a few kilometers from the Ontario and Manitoba borders in Canada. My mother had moved there after being widowed and rebuilding her life with Bart, who sadly passed away months after the pandemic ended, from causes unrelated to the virus.

So I packed our bags, gathered my three little chicks, closed the house, and left for Pengilly.

Just the change of environment helped me see things from a different perspective.

It was there that gratitude —as I mentioned earlier— would take a leading role, not just in my life, but in the method I would later channel, and I was finally able to see the challenges as opportunities for growth.

The lockdown forced me to grieve the divorce without external distractions, without outings to clear my head, or other people's hugs to console me.

This time, there was no escape.

I couldn't avoid the pain.

Alcohol wasn't an option. In my family, I had witnessed destructive behaviors tied to its abuse —me included— and I knew that waking up hungover while caring for three children under the age of eight was anything but wise.

During my first grief, after my father's death, I turned to alcohol to numb the pain… and it didn't work.

My mom also fell victim to it on several occasions, and it was painful to understand that you can't help someone who isn't ready to heal.

This time, with three small lives depending on me, I had to choose differently.

Luckily, I had help at home and my basic needs were covered: food, shelter, support.

I was in a beautiful place, surrounded by trees, silence, and nature.

I saw in that environment the perfect opportunity to reconnect with my inner world.

An ideal place to heal from the inside, far from noise, from social pressure, and above all, from the constant need to interact with the human species.

Unlike that grief from two decades ago, this time I didn't take refuge in the outside.

I had to go inward.

And in the midst of the blessed darkness, the light began to show.

There are moments when everything seems to collapse. When you feel empty, broken, alone.

But it's right there, in that space of silence, where the most sacred begins to reveal itself: **your essence.**

That's what happened to me in Pengilly.

After the storm of the divorce, the emotional chaos, the deep grief, and the global pandemic that followed, **my soul began to surrender.**

Not in the sense of giving up on life, but in **surrendering to the process.**

I began to let go of the character, the masks, the rigidity of having to know it all… and little by little, I began to remember who I was.

I was in a cozy cabin, in a town almost invisible on the map, surrounded by melting snow, lakes, and pines.

There, without makeup, without filters, without stages or agendas, I realized that this darkness was sacred, that this challenge came with a reward.

And it was then that I began **to receive.**

One March night, at the start of the pandemic, when it was time for bed, Diego, my eldest son, came up to me and asked:

—Mom, why are we in Pengilly and not in McAllen or with Dad?

How do you explain to an eight-year-old what a global pandemic is, a marital crisis, and an emotional breakdown... when you yourself don't fully understand what's happening?

Then I heard an inner voice say:

"Write a poem."

And that's what we did.

We all lay down together in one bed, and amid hugs, tears, and laughter, this was born:

〜

A Kingdom With More Wisdom

At first it was a mystery,
Something never seen in history!
It felt like a vacation
But locked down, no question!
A few weeks passed before we realized,
That our whole system was paralyzed.
Anxiety kept growing,
And straight answers were not flowing.
We tried to stay optimistic
Find a hobby, get realistic!
Our mood swings made us sweat
Leaving home, we would regret.
Some nights we end up crying,
This is serious, I'm not lying!
Then wake up and get some action,
Cook or play, find a distraction!

But since this will take a while,
And we need more reasons to smile,
We must get real
And figure out a way to heal.
Because this must be a sign,
To wake up and align:
So we remember how to love,
And feel the magic of a hug.
With our hearts communicate,
And having a job, appreciate.
Value the beauty nature lays,
So kids play in fun new ways
To show respect for all mankind
And leave all illnesses behind.

Then we'll be happy to say, while we gratefully pray, that we come from a
kingdom with more wisdom!

~

We all went to bed, in peace.

The next morning I decided to recite it on my social media. It went viral.

It was published in media outlets, shared on social networks, I was interviewed to talk about it and how it had come about during the lockdown.

I began receiving messages from all over the world; people thanking me for putting into words something they too were living but didn't know how to express.

It was my first clear sign:

I was ready to share from my process, not from perfection.

And it was precisely from one of those interviews that the universe sent me another surprise.

One of those you don't expect, but that arrives with purpose.

One night, after a live Instagram interview, I received a message from someone who had seen the broadcast where I spoke about the poem.

"Thank you for sharing that poem. You're such a badass."

CHAPTER FOUR
A NEW LOVE?

That message was the starting point.

I didn't know who he was because his Instagram account was private and didn't show his name.

So it wasn't logic — it was my intuition that accepted the friend request.

And when his identity was revealed, I was pleasantly surprised.

We started texting back and forth, with ease, with respect, with honesty... and with a familiar energy that felt deeply comforting.

Talking to him was like talking to a forgotten part of myself.

A soul that saw my soul.

A mirror without judgment.

Soon, he became my long-distance confidant.

A conversation partner I could talk to about everything: love, God, pain, my dreams, my finances, my projects, even my most intimate fears.

His presence was medicine.

Most of the time we communicated by video call; we liked seeing each other, and that made us feel closer.

While he was at the South Pole and I at the North Pole, the connection felt as if we were face to face.

Mauricio —whom I nicknamed, in my mind and in my heart, "**Mau Wow**"— came into my life with such perfect, unexpected, and precise synchronicity that there was no other way to describe it.

He was a gift disguised as friendship, sent straight from heaven.

He was a wow—inside and out.

A true **heartthrob**, or **papacito**, as we Colombians say, with a deep gaze revealed in his beautiful green eyes, a flirty and cheeky sense of humor, an authentic masculinity, and a gentlemanliness that made me feel valued.

Structured, decent, special.

A rare gem.

And yes, God sent me a Colombian, as proof that my romantic traumas with my fellow countrymen had already been healed.

A confirmation that life goes on, that the heart can feel again, and that there are still surprises waiting for you when you decide to heal and open up.

If it were up to me, I'd have married him the next day.

But I knew Mauricio wasn't here for that.

He came to help me climb out of the hole, to remind me of my worth, and to lift me toward the vast.

His role was clear: to be a bridge, not a destination.

With him, I experienced a deep vibrational shift in my grief process.

I went from seeing myself as a broken woman to recognizing myself as a woman in rebirth.

A woman who could dream again.

Who didn't have to settle.

Who deserved so much more.

It was as if the universe whispered to me:

"Relax, girl, there are more than eight billion people in the world, and yes... there are more handsome, more intelligent, more successful, and more evolved ones out there. Just wait until you recover your self-worth, your sense of deserving... and believe it."

We saw each other twice.

The first time, in Chicago.

Yes, it sounded crazy: traveling alone to meet someone I'd never seen physically, in an unfamiliar city.

But Mauricio wasn't a stranger to my soul.

It felt like a long-awaited reunion.

As if our souls were saying to each other in unison:

"At last, I've found you again."

The first time we met was at the airport.

My flight arrived a few minutes before his, so I picked up my suitcase and leaned against the baggage claim wall, sweating from nerves, wearing my mask, and with my heart racing a mile a minute.

Suddenly, I got a message:

"Where are you?"

His flight had already landed, and he was getting closer.

"Here!" I replied.

And when I least expected it, he was already in front of me.

We looked each other straight in the eyes, hiding the smile of emotion and nerves under our masks.

—And now? —he asked, with a soft laugh, as if the answer were already floating between us.

I stepped closer, gently removed his mask with trembling tenderness, took off mine, and with sweet determination, I kissed him.

A kiss that didn't ask for permission, that didn't need words, because it had already said everything.

Being with Mau Wow was magical and liberating.

Little by little, I began to realize what I truly wanted in a partner.

My brain took notes while my heart expanded with gratitude.

He showed me, without knowing it, the kind of treatment I deserved, and gave me the clarity I needed to know exactly what to ask the universe for.

After that, the bar was set high.

Very high.

I would no longer settle for just anything.

Whoever came into my life would have to exceed that level.

Even though we both knew that it might be the first and only time we'd see each other.

I had many things to sort out upon returning to McAllen, and neither distance nor circumstances were on our side.

Still, we both knew that our connection was forever.

But the story didn't end there.

Life, with its mysterious sense of timing, had a new chapter in store.

A year later, our paths crossed again.

And this time, in Mexico City.

A short encounter, but profoundly special.

We wandered, we laughed, we ate delicious food.

And then, hand in hand, we went together to visit the Virgin of Guadalupe.

There, before her, we gave thanks for so much.

For what we had lived.

For what we had felt.

For the miracle of having crossed paths in this life.

For the mission fulfilled.

I could already feel it: I knew that could be the last time I'd see him in person.

There was something in the air, in our glances, in that lingering hug before saying goodbye… that confirmed to me the earthly cycle was ending there.

My process had made a quantum leap.

He had been the perfect catalyst, and his part of the soul agreement was now complete.

I openly acknowledge, with a full heart, that he was — and still is — one of those earthly angels who arrive at the exact moment to remind you of your greatness, to help you rebuild, and to show you, with tenderness, that life still holds gifts yet to be discovered.

That cosmic encounter marked a before and after.

His arrival shook me, lifted me, reminded me who I was, and awakened something in me.

A new love?

Not one to stay.

But yes — one to give me the most important love of all: self-love.

CHAPTER FIVE
THE DOWNLOADS

The downloads didn't stop.

What followed was a true cascade of messages, ideas, and complete structures.

They arrived with a clarity that gave me chills.

I felt peace and, at the same time, excitement knowing I was having direct communication with the 99%.

I understood that when I was in that state of harmony and peace, when I was vibrating high, I could connect with the source without interference.

What had changed was my energy: I had activated an internal antenna capable of finally tuning in to the voice of my higher self.

It was a subtle, everyday, sacred process.

I surrendered.

I gave myself over to silence, to gratitude, to nature.

I stopped fighting what I didn't understand and started observing it with love.

Walking through the forest, listening to my breath, writing out all that hurt, giving thanks even without knowing what was coming... it all became part of the path.

I let go of the need to understand everything.

I let go of the strong persona.

I let go of the urgency to control.

I began to pray more.

To talk to my angels.

To enjoy coffee, to dance.

To ask for signs... and to recognize them.

To trust that life was holding me, even in the midst of chaos.

Pure high-frequency stuff.

One early morning, without seeking it, I channeled the structure of what I would later call **Letter to the Universe:**

a clear, spiritual, and deeply practical process for manifesting from the soul.

A program born to help others — and also myself — remember the power we have when we dare to live from our authenticity.

Without knowing it, I was already downloading the R's that would later become the heart of my methodology.

I understood something crucial:

I can't manifest anything if I don't know what I want... but even less if I don't feel I deserve it.

Boom! A secret unlocked.

To manifest, it's not enough to have clarity; you need to feel that what you desire is not impossible, that it's already yours, that it always has been.

But to reach that level of certainty, **you must level up.**

You must become the version of you who already has it.

And to become that version of me, I had to reprogram many beliefs and heal deep traumas that were limiting and blocking my path.

Of course, it's a process.

A methodology.

As I was having realization after realization, scattered messages began to arrive, like whispers from heaven.

I felt like I was on a secret mission, and that formulas were being revealed to me to make quantum leaps without having to start over from scratch.

Was I imagining it… or was I going crazy?

The prayers, the phrases, the affirmations found me.

They appeared while I walked in the snow, while I meditated, while I wrote.

They were words that spoke directly to my heart.

I began to write them down, one by one, in my notebook.

Without planning it, that notebook began to turn into a guide.

That's how **The Universe Speaks** was born.

The oracle.

The divine orders that were guiding me at every step of the process.

But… why was this happening to me?

As far as I can remember, I'd never had contact with "the beyond," nor was I clairvoyant or anything like that.

What changed?

"Your frequency is elevated.

You are vibrating from love, acceptance, gratitude, abundance, and peace.

IT'S NOT MAGIC; IT'S FREQUENCY."

That was the answer.

The consequence of my surrender.

Of my willingness to see with new eyes.

But, as universal laws are perfect and never fail, with this discovery and realization amid such a sacred process, the inevitable balance also arrived.

The law of polarity had to manifest… and the reality of the 1% came knocking at my door.

That 1% —the physical, visible, dense plane— came to remind me that there were still trials to face, emotions to integrate, and challenges to overcome.

Because even though my soul was already vibrating in the 99%, I still inhabited a human body full of stories, wounds, and struggles.

And the universe, in its wisdom, invited me to apply everything I had learned… in **tangible reality.**

I still didn't know how I was going to face life after the pandemic.

I was in a healing bubble, reorganizing my thoughts, digesting emotions, and holding my children with presence.

But I knew that, sooner or later, I would have to return to the real world:

—getting a job, buying a car, paying bills…

—and supporting ourselves without relying on a limited pension converted into dollars.

And that, clearly, was not sustainable.

My stepfather, with the best intentions —but from his logic— told me:

—Apply to any job, even if it's at Home Depot or Walmart.

Here in the United States, you have nothing, and you are nobody.

You are poor and you have to start from the bottom.

The only thing I can do for you is lend you money for a second-hand car.

You pay it back little by little… but you have to sign a promissory note.

His words hit me like a kick to the soul —not to mention the butt—.

But instead of letting that knock me down, a voice inside me ignited strongly:

"That is not my destiny.

I can write another story."

Yes, I had doubts. Of course.

But I also had **proof.**

Living proof that whenever I aligned with intention, **things happened.**

Not because I had degrees, contacts, or qualifications.

But because of my burning desire. Because of my attitude. Because of my energy.

And from that place —from the "North Pole," as we affectionately call Pengilly— I manifested, against all odds, the job that would mark the beginning of my new life: an interview with a businessman in McAllen who was waiting for me upon my return to Texas, just in time to receive my green card and be able to work legally.

That meeting would be the starting point to take the reins of my professional life, stabilize myself first, and then continue with my legacy and life purpose.

Nothing I experienced in Pengilly —the poem, the program, the oracle, the connection, the healing— was isolated.

Everything was part of the same sacred fabric: a process of returning to my center, elevating my frequency enough to receive what I truly came to share.

And although at that moment I was just going through it, later I would see it with total clarity:

All those channeled tools were pieces of the same code.

That code became the heart of my practice.

The map I had already traveled without knowing it.

Because there are truths you don't learn: **you remember.**

And there are methods you don't design: **you embody.**

That's what I did:

I embodied my own method without knowing it was being born.

The 5R Method.

And with it, the beginning of the path that would change my life.

And that of many others.

CHAPTER SIX

THE 5R METHOD OF MANIFESTATION

The energetic path to your new reality

This method is not a theory. It is a mental, energetic, emotional, and spiritual practice.

It helps you manifest what you desire —a healthy relationship, a new home, professional clarity, well-being, inner peace, abundance— from the roots.

You can apply it at any moment in your life.

For an urgent change or a deep transformation.

For big decisions or daily adjustments.

To reconnect with yourself, unblock, and manifest from your truth.

RECOGNIZE. RESET. REDIRECT. REBUILD. RECLAIM.

Five steps.

Five keys.

Five inner movements that transform your frequency… and with it, your reality.

~

RECOGNIZE

What do I want? Who am I?

(Connect with your true desire and your authentic identity)

I had to admit that I was living a life I hadn't consciously chosen.

I was in the middle of a painful divorce, raising three children alone, without a support network or financial certainty.

I landed in McAllen by circumstance, not choice.

I thought I wanted to go to Austin, Miami, or Barranquilla, but the truth is that I just wanted to run. Run from my pain. From my chaos. From my loneliness.

I had no idea what I truly wanted. I only knew I didn't want to keep living like that.

Not because of a lack of options, but because of a lack of clarity. And fear. A lot of fear.

And I'm not the only one.

It seems simple, but the truth is most people don't know what they want. And not because they're indecisive, but because they've spent years disconnected from themselves.

Living in survival mode, fulfilling others' expectations, following inherited scripts, prioritizing what they *should* want instead of what they truly desire.

Maybe they know what they *don't* want —what hurts, what's uncomfortable, what limits them— but when someone asks: "What do *you* want?", they go blank.

. . .

Not because they don't have dreams, but because they forgot how to listen to themselves.

Not because they don't want anything, but because they can't see beyond their story, their environment, or their limiting beliefs.

They want a better life, but it feels out of reach.

They see it as a luxury reserved for others.

And their inner dialogue is stuck in lack. In complaints. In what's missing.

In everything that keeps them from seeing themselves clearly.

Because recognizing what you truly want isn't easy when you don't even recognize yourself.

~

WHAT THE HELL DO YOU WANT?

Imagine you're at a restaurant.

There are two kinds of people: those who know exactly what they're going to order... and those who have no idea.

They know they're hungry, sure, but they don't know what for.

And when you don't know what you want, someone else decides for you, you order what the person next to you is having, or you just accept whatever they bring. And you end up eating what was there — not what you truly craved.

Now let's take it a step further: choosing the restaurant.

Some people know from the start they want sushi, pasta, or a burger.

And others spend hours searching for options, doubting, asking, comparing... and still don't choose.

That indecision isn't random: it reflects someone who's lost touch with their desire.

Now picture another scene: you're at the airport, ready to travel.

You get to the counter and the agent asks you:

"—Destination?"

And you answer:

"—I don't know… I just want to get out of here."

That's how most people live.

Wanting to escape what they don't like, but without any clarity about where they want to go.

And when you don't know your destination, any flight seems like a good one.

But you can also end up somewhere you don't want to be, just because you didn't know how to choose.

When you know what to order, where you are, and where you're going… the Universe also knows how to deliver it.

To recognize is exactly that.

It's having clarity before you place your order.

It's knowing your destination before you board the plane.

It's choosing from awareness, not reaction.

To recognize is to know where you want to live.

What kind of partner you're looking for.

How much money you want to generate each month.

What lifestyle excites you.

And who you want to become.

To recognize is to shine light on the root.

And once you shine that light… there's no going back.

You start remembering what you want.

You start remembering who you are.

It's not about imagining what *would* be nice.

It's about being brutally honest with yourself.

Knowing that if you can recognize it, if you can imagine it, if you can see it clearly… you can manifest it too.

Because if it exists in your mind, it's because it already exists in some line of reality.

To recognize is having the courage to look honestly at where you are,

but also to visualize where you're going.

It's remembering that the version of you who already has what you dream of… already exists.

It's simply vibrating at another frequency. And your job is to get closer to it.

To recognize also means knowing your core values, your non-negotiables.

Because once you know those, decision-making becomes easy, and doubt doesn't show up.

You become someone who chooses from faith, not fear.

And everything, absolutely everything, starts to change from there.

And that's where the next R comes in: **RESET.**

Because once you recognize what you want —or at the very least, what you're no longer willing to tolerate— you need to clear the path.

Empty your mind of everything that ever told you that you couldn't.

Release the voices that planted fear, doubt, or guilt.

Question the beliefs that aren't yours, but that you've carried as if they were.

To reset is the moment you confirm what you DO want… but this time, without limitations.

∽

RESET

What is holding me back?

(Identify and release beliefs and emotions that limit you)

Once you recognize your emotions, what you want —or what you're definitely no longer willing to tolerate— it's time to make space.

To cleanse, to release, to reprogram.

Because if you keep thinking the same, believing the same, reacting the same… you'll keep manifesting the same.

Resetting is the second step of the method.

It's not enough to know what you want if you're still vibrating at the frequency of what you fear.

And to shift your frequency, you need to question your most deeply rooted beliefs.

Not with judgment, but with awareness.

Resetting isn't about forgetting what you've lived.

It's not about covering pain with empty affirmations.

It's not about pretending you're okay when you're filled with fear inside.

It's about facing your belief system head-on and asking: IS IT TRUE?

- Where does this story I'm telling myself come from?
- Who told me I couldn't?
- Since when did I believe I had to settle?

I, for example, had a very well-written story in my head: *"McAllen is not a good place to live."*

It felt small, limited, unfamiliar. I hadn't chosen it.

I ended up there because of the circumstances of my divorce.

And with that came another heavy thought: *"I'm going to have to do everything alone."*

Three children under eight, no family nearby, no support network, no idea how I was going to handle it all.

That's what I believed.

And like everything you believe, you project.

So at first, all I could see was what was missing.

But that's when I had to apply the tool.

That's when the second R came in: **Reset.**

I had to change my perception.

I had to rewrite the story.

I had to stop looking at what was limiting me… and start seeing what was supporting me.

And everything began to shift.

I began to imagine a new story.

One in which I could make new friends through my kids' schools.

One in which those friendships could become a closer support network.

I thought maybe I could find a live-in nanny, taking advantage of being close to Mexico.

That the job I had manifested from that interview could give me stability.

I started to see that I didn't even have to speak English, because most people were bilingual — even leaning more toward Spanish.

And that visiting family in Austin or Houston was as simple as driving a few hours.

None of that had happened yet.

But for the first time... **I saw it as possible.**

And that changed everything.

I began transforming every phrase that kept me stuck.

I changed *"I have to stay in McAllen"* to *"I'm choosing to be here temporarily while I build something better."*

I changed *"this is all I have"* to *"this job is a platform to move forward, not my final destination."*

I changed *"I have nothing"* to *"I'm starting over with wisdom I didn't have before."*

It wasn't magic.

It was a decision.

It was faith.

It was awareness.

Resetting is that.

It's opening Pandora's box of your mind and deciding which thoughts stay, which no longer serve you, and what new story you're going to create.

Without acting from fear or guilt.

Without repeating inherited patterns.

Without living in debt to everything and everyone.

Resetting isn't about erasing your past.

It's about rewriting the meaning you gave it.

It's looking straight at what's blocking you…

and transforming it into what propels you forward.

You can't build a new life with an old operating system.

You need to update your mind to the version of you that already has what you desire.

Do you want an abundant life?

You can't keep believing that money is dirty.

Do you want a healthy relationship?

You can't keep thinking that love always hurts.

Do you want to manifest something big?

Then start seeing yourself as big too.

Resetting is choosing, again and again, thoughts that bring you closer to your vision.

It's stopping feeding the fear and beginning to nourish faith.

It's stopping the internal repetition of *"I can't…"*

and starting to tell yourself:

What if I can?

Because your mind is the filter of your reality.

And when you clean the filter… **everything changes.**

~

REDIRECT

How do I want to feel, and where do I want to go?

(Raise your frequency first, plant the right emotion, and redirect your energy toward your new vision)

With a new mindset and a revamped "subconscious operating and hacking system," the next step was inevitable: choosing where I wanted to go.

Because recognizing what you want is one thing—and internally preparing to support it is another.

Redirecting isn't about running impulsively.

Nor is it about staying still and waiting.

It's that moment when your energy aligns with your vision, and everything begins to take direction.

Here, you don't just think differently—you begin to feel differently.

Here, you start feeling differently.

You're no longer asking, "Will it happen?"

You hold the certainty that it is possible.

You begin to visualize.

You write your letter to the universe.

You create your vision board.

You start feeling in tune with what once seemed distant.

And from that elevated frequency, **you prepare.**

Redirecting is that: **the energetic preparation before the birth of the new.**

It involves action, yes—but internal, powerful, and strategic.

With the ground cleared and beliefs reset, my energy was ready to plant a new direction.

It wasn't impulse... it was a vibrational choice.

Like when a company prepares to launch a campaign.

Nothing has been published yet, but the branding is already being designed, the messaging is being refined, the team is being organized.

Everything is aligning behind the scenes.

In my case, that was the moment I stopped focusing on what was missing and started visualizing a different life.

I imagined myself surrounded by people who elevated my energy, doing work that inspired me, with time for my kids—and for myself too.

And from that vision, I began to prepare.

To redirect is to create vibrational structure.

It's the moment when your intention begins to turn into direction.

Your energy becomes your strategy.

And the plan is born from your frequency, not from pressure.

You don't need to know how it will arrive.

You only need to be aligned with what you want to receive.

In the restaurant example:

To recognize is knowing what you want to order.

To reset is releasing the doubt about whether you deserve it. *Is it too expensive? Will it upset my stomach? Is it okay to treat myself to this?*

. . .

But in **Redirecting**, you've already made the decision.

You already know what you're going to order—and you're savoring it.

In a pregnancy, redirecting would be preparing for the baby's arrival.

You've already felt life begin inside you.

It hasn't arrived yet, but you're already vibrating in its existence.

You decorate the room, pack the hospital bag, choose the name, clear space in your calendar—and you see it coming.

It's a reality for you.

You feel overwhelming emotion.

Redirecting is having clarity without rigidity.

It's preparing without forcing.

It's feeling it as real before seeing it manifested.

It's trusting that your energy is the soil… and the manifestation, the harvest.

And right when everything is ready on the inside…

when you're already holding it with certainty and without anxiety…

comes the moment to take aligned action with your vision.

That's the next R:

REBUILD!

～

REBUILD

How does my best self act?

(Start thinking, feeling, and acting as if you had already manifested your dream.)

. . .

Because I had recognized my worth, reset my fears, and redirected my energy, I was ready to act from my most authentic self.

To rebuild is when energy turns into matter.

It's when you stop imagining the life you want—and start living it.

This is where your transformation is confirmed.

It's no longer enough to have clarity or to feel that it's possible.

You have to walk like someone who already has it.

You have to make decisions from the place you want to arrive at—not from the one you're leaving behind.

To rebuild means:

Act like someone who already is.

Like someone who already has what they asked for.

Like someone who is ready to hold what's coming.

And it's not about pretending or faking it.

It's about moving from a real frequency.

You speak differently.

You think differently.

You make different decisions.

In my case, it was when the interview in McAllen came through.

I didn't show up from a place of lack, nor from the need to be chosen.

I went as a woman who knows her worth.

I didn't ask for a position—I offered a solution.

I proposed a collaboration.

And just like that, we created a role tailored to my life at that moment.

That day, I didn't get a job.

That day, I confirmed that I was already operating from a new version of myself.

That's what rebuilding is:

Confirming with your actions what your energy had already declared.

Making decisions that align with your new identity.

Choosing from expansion, not from fear.

From possibility, not from habit.

You don't need to transform your life overnight.

You just need to act like someone who has already crossed the bridge.

Even if the path isn't fully built yet.

Rebuilding is when you place your order.

It's when you look at the waiter, say confidently what you want, and know it's going to arrive.

You don't question it.

You don't repeat it with doubt.

You don't wonder if they understood.

You simply... asked for it.

Rebuilding is holding your new frequency through your decisions.

It's turning vision into action.

It's doing new things from who you already are—not from who you used to be.

It's presence.

It's congruence.

It's identity in motion.

When you rebuild, you're not trying.

You're embodying.

And that… changes everything.

〜

RECLAIM

Am I open to receiving everything, without controlling the how?

(Let go of control and trust that you will receive your manifestation.)

Once you've recognized it, cleared it, visualized it, and started living it… the quietest and most powerful moment arrives: the moment of letting go.

Because even though it might seem simple, often the hardest part isn't manifesting…

it's allowing yourself to receive what's already knocking at your door.

To reclaim isn't to demand from the universe.

It's to say, with humility: **"I'm ready."**

It's opening up to receive what you asked for—and more.

Without minimizing it.

Without thinking you don't deserve it.

Without sabotaging it with impatience, fear, or the need to control everything.

• • •

This step isn't about doing more.

It's about letting go.

Letting go of control, obsession, anxiety.

Letting go of the *"when?"*, the *"how?"*, the *"will it really happen?"*

And staying in the right frequency—even when the form hasn't shown up yet.

Because you've already done your part.

You've already planted the seed.

You've already cleared the way.

You've already aligned yourself.

You've already acted like the person you are.

Now, the only thing left… is to open your arms.

In the restaurant example:

You recognized what you wanted, let go of doubt, decided with clarity, and ordered with certainty.

Reclaiming is that moment when you've already placed the order, and instead of checking if they're preparing it, you simply wait… knowing it's on its way.

You relax.

You enjoy the company.

You sip your water calmly.

You *know* it's coming.

Not because you see it, but because you already ordered it with certainty.

. . .

To reclaim is to live that way.

It's trusting as if it were already here.

It's giving thanks in advance.

It's allowing yourself to celebrate before holding it in your hands.

And it was right there—when I let go—that the offer arrived.

A tailor-made job, with the flexibility I needed to still care for my children.

It was exactly what I needed at that moment.

Because the universe responds.

It was frequency.

The natural result of being aligned with everything I had planted from the soul.

Reclaiming is the most sacred moment.

You're not waiting.

You're receiving.

And that is done with presence.

With gratitude.

With faith.

Because when you recognize, reset, redirect, rebuild... and let go, what you once dreamed of begins to manifest before your very eyes.

Everything begins to arrive.

And the moment to receive it...

is now.

This method wasn't something I learned in a course.

Life dictated it to me.

My soul channeled it.

My experience confirmed it.

CHAPTER SEVEN

THE TRIPLE D AND THE AWAKENING

This process of rebirth wasn't my first awakening.

When I lived in Miami in the early 2000s, I plunged into something like an awakening… but in reverse.

I was alive, but disconnected.

I was searching for myself, but in the wrong place.

After my father died, immaturely and ignorantly, I began a frantic search, trying to fill the emptiness through absolutely everything external: parties, shopping, food, drugs, alcohol, sex… everything that, ironically, distances you further from yourself and from God.

It was the true Triple D —a name my college friends and I gave that stage of emotional and existential chaos: **Disorder, Disaster, and Dishevelment.**

Today, looking back, I add a fourth D: **Despertar** (Awakening).

Because without living through all of that, I wouldn't be here today telling you this story.

I don't regret it, but I do recognize that I lost precious years chasing outside what I could only find within.

I was exposed.

Vulnerable.

Thirsty for belonging.

Wanting to be rescued by something or someone.

I witnessed the most ostentatious, wild, and decadent parties you can imagine.

I remember one particularly dark night, drenched in flickering lights and blaring music, where I ended up —without knowing how— in Versace's old mansion.

Surrounded by intoxicated people, entangled bodies, and dense energy, I witnessed an orgy scene for the first time that left me stunned, scared, and wanting to run.

And that's what I did.

But the most striking thing wasn't the escape—**it was *who* helped me leave.**

The friend I arrived with introduced me to his boss, a Colombian entrepreneur.

Upon hearing my name, he stared at me and asked:

—*What is your relation to Kico Chams?*

I nearly had a heart attack.

—*He was my father*, I replied.

His eyes widened in surprise.

—*Your dad was my roommate in college!*

In that moment, I knew my father was there.

Watching over me.

Confirming I wasn't alone.

That even in the darkest places, light finds you.

That man, who could have been just another stranger, became an angel.

He gave me $100 and a kiss on the forehead.

Just like my dad used to do.

And he said:

—*Go home.*

I got into the taxi with my heart racing.

When I arrived at my building, the driver had no change.

In that moment of confusion, a young man who urgently needed to get to the airport approached and said:

—*I got you, I'll pay for your taxi, because I'm in a rush and mine hasn't arrived.*

I was left holding a $100 bill, ready to be spent on more partying, but with a sense of satisfaction and gratitude: **I had received a sign from Kico Chams, my guardian angel—and I was $100 richer.**

Another night, equally or even more dangerous, I got a call from a Brazilian couple I'd met months earlier at a party. Unbeknownst to me, they were swingers, and their intentions were clear.

We met for drinks, and they offered me a margarita. What I didn't know was that they'd laced it with **angel dust**—a highly potent dissociative drug.

With the first sip, my free will dissolved.

I lost control. I became someone I didn't recognize. And though the friends I'd arrived with tried to stop me, I ended up at the couple's apartment.

CAROLINA CHAMS

But once again, **another angel appeared**—this time disguised as a housekeeper who happened to show up that very day to clean. Her arrival sparked an argument between them, giving me a moment of clarity.

I managed to contact my roommate, who had been desperately trying to find me all night. She rushed to get me.

And just like that, I was saved. Again.

It was precisely after that experience that I knew—without a doubt:

Something had to change.

I couldn't keep going with the flow.

I couldn't keep searching for answers in relationships that only drained me or in places that only fueled my disconnection.

I'd had enough disorder, disaster, and dishevelment.

It was time to choose something different.

It was time to choose awakening.

One night, I went out without really wanting to—just to appease my friends. I sat down on a speaker and stayed there, watching people as if my body was present, but my soul was not.

That same night, Kike and Gabi showed up—two new friends.

They approached me, we talked, danced, and the night ended with an after-party at my place.

During those early hours, Gabi leaned in and dropped a sentence that sparked my curiosity:

—*Mamacita, you've got Unity right next door. Have you been there?*

He explained that Unity was a spiritual center offering meditation classes, just a few blocks from where I lived.

We agreed to go meditate together that same week.

His stage name was **Gabriel Archangel.**

56

His profession: photographer.

Yes—**Archangel.**

That's how, in one of the most disoriented moments of my life, the universe sent me Gabriel.

Not just the human, but the celestial one too.

Gabriel, the divine messenger.

The archangel who, according to spiritual traditions, announces births, rebirths, truths that awaken, and paths that reveal themselves when you're ready to see them.

Gabriel—the one who shows up to tell you:

It's time.

And what did he announce to me?

My awakening.

Because when the soul is ready, the messengers appear.

Not always with wings.

Sometimes with a camera hanging from their neck, a kind gaze, and a name you simply can't overlook.

Thanks to that encounter — with both the earthly Gabriel and the spiritual one — I understood that everything I had been looking for in parties and chaos... **had always been within me.**

At **Unity on the Bay**, I met my first teachers in personal and spiritual development: **Louise Hay and Wayne Dyer.**

Their words opened my eyes. They taught me to love myself, to forgive myself, to speak to myself kindly, to hold myself with compassion.

It was also there that I discovered the book **The Secret.**

And although I now know that manifestation runs far deeper than what that book simplifies, it was my first contact with the idea that **I could create my reality.**

My healing journey didn't start with incense or yoga.

It started with a taxi.

An emotional overdose.

A kiss on the forehead.

And an angel named Gabriel.

That was my awakening.

Not a glamorous or mystical one.

It was real. Raw. Chaotic.

Triple D. Disorder. Disaster. Disarray.

And then, yes: **Awakening.**

CHAPTER EIGHT
LETTER TO THE UNIVERSE

Just before meeting Jorge and marrying him, I did an experiment that became a turning point in my life: I wrote my first **"Letter to the Universe,"** in which I detailed exactly what I was looking for in a partner.

The Triple D phase was nearing its end, and with all my being I longed for a serious, stable relationship.

So I applied some tools based on the Law of Attraction, which suggests that our thoughts and emotions hold the power to draw experiences and situations into our lives.

According to this law, if we focus on what we desire and maintain a positive mindset, we can manifest those desires into our reality.

Everything in the universe is energy, and like attracts like.

However, there was one aspect I hadn't yet mastered: the premise I later discovered in my own methodology.

It was crucial to check whether my desire was coming from lack or from a state of abundance.

This is key, because at that moment—when I manifested Jorge—my desires were rooted in lack.

I was longing to be rescued, and when you manifest from that place, you inevitably attract more reasons to feel empty.

No one is going to complete you; you have to feel complete first, and from that place attract someone who truly complements you.

So I wrote (from my emptiness) but with deep emotion:

> Dear Universe,
>
> Thank you for blessing me with a full life—true friendships, a stable job, and a supportive family.
> Thank you for bringing into my life my soulmate: a cultured and generous man, intelligent and charming.
> I love his smile and his way of being. He speaks Portuguese, he's not from Barranquilla, he's a foreigner.
> He enjoys parties but is also responsible in business. He sees me as a princess, and I learn so much from him.
> I am ready now to have a healthy relationship with someone who will take care of me and protect me.
> Physical appearance doesn't matter to me, only that he loves me.
> I trust he will arrive soon.
>
> It is done,
> Carolina Chams

A few weeks later, I met Jorge.

And he was exactly what I asked for: a cultured, generous, intelligent, and charming man.

With a pleasant smile, he spoke Portuguese, he wasn't from Barranquilla but from Mexico, he liked to party, was hardworking, and treated me like a princess.

Though physically he wasn't my type, the chemistry between us was undeniable.

Exactly what I had requested.

So what happened next?

I married the person I was meant to marry.

There were too many "godincidences" in our relationship.

We both studied at the same university, moved to Miami after graduating, had a sibling of the opposite sex, our mothers shared the same name (Catalina), and my father and he had a name swap: Jorge Alberto and Alberto Jorge.

Plus, Jorge was a Scorpio—something that had marked my life from the beginning.

I had a birthmark on my leg that, over the years, took the shape of a scorpion.

When I discovered my birthmark, I ran to show it to my mom, frustrated, and I said:

—*"How do I get rid of this? A scorpion, how ugly!"*

My mom, quick-witted, replied:

—*"Oh Caro! That means you're going to marry a Scorpio."*

And there it was: the manifestation in all its splendor.

That idea became a deeply rooted belief in my subconscious, and that's exactly what I attracted. It's not magic—it's science.

I met Jorge through Juani and Andrés, better known as "La Rata."

These Mexicans were part of Jorge's friend group in Miami.

Since I was ready to meet people from other nationalities, I fell for it completely, as they say in Mexico.

I met Andrés first, on the same day Jorge was celebrating his master's graduation in Political Science at the University of Miami.

The friend group had split—some were in one club, others in another. I ran into Andrés where Jorge wasn't.

We became friends, and from that day forward, we were inseparable.

After his studies ended, Jorge returned to Ciudad del Carmen to help his parents with their oil business.

So our paths crossed again—since we had actually overlapped at UT years earlier during shared classes.

Months later, La Rata and Juani said, "We want to introduce you to your future husband," and that's how I found Jorge on Facebook.

We started chatting, and cleverly, one day he said Mexico and Colombia were playing a soccer match and suggested a bet:

—*"If Mexico wins, you invite me to dinner at Sushi Samba; if Colombia wins, I'll invite you."*

While chatting long-distance with the new internet technology, I realized I was losing interest in partying.

Yes, I was losing the desire to party!

This man had me completely hooked.

And indeed, when Colombia won (a major ego boost), Jorge replied:

—*"Betting debts are honorable debts; I'll be there next week."*

And the rest is history.

He came to settle his bet, and over aguardientes, tequilas, and songs, our beautiful long-distance relationship began.

It was a short courtship—the distance didn't last long once Jorge convinced me to spend a few months in Mexico to "see if it would work."

I decided quickly, without fear of change.

It was, in part, that same emptiness that had led me there.

I sold my things, quit my job, and went for it.

A few months passed, and during that trial period, a special moment arrived.

It was February 14th, and the excitement of the day overwhelmed me as we left the island early to begin a road trip to Hacienda Uayamon.

This place, located in Campeche, was a 19th-century agricultural estate known for henequen production.

The hacienda had been restored into a boutique hotel, blending historic charm with modern comforts.

We stopped at Isla Aguada for a panuchos breakfast, then in Champotón for a shrimp cocktail lunch, before arriving at Uayamon for dinner.

On the road, the music shifted—from rancheras in his honor, to vallenato for me, with some bossa nova, '80s and '90s hits, and Spanish rock.

I must confess: when it came to music, he was "the one."

His gifted voice captivated me whenever he picked up the guitar— without trying to steal the show.

He did it naturally, and it was enchanting.

Upon arrival, I was enveloped by the beauty of its colonial architecture and lush gardens—a retreat promising a unique, enriching experience as we began a new chapter in our relationship.

We toured the gardens, the spa, and the terrace cabin that would witness that special night.

But something wasn't right.

Before dinner, a brutal migraine began to rise, threatening to ruin the evening.

That migraine may have been a cosmic clue to alert me—but amid the excitement, I ignored the sign.

We opted for a couples' massage at the spa to unwind before dinner, and after, resumed the romantic evening.

Everything seemed perfect, atmosphere filled with anticipation.

But as the night progressed, the migraine persisted, and a slight anxiety crept in.

At the table, we toasted champagne, letting its bubbles surround us— though part of me still felt uneasy.

Then the waiter appeared, and upon hearing his name I felt a chill:

—*"Alberto."*

Everything started to make sense.

The waiter assigned to us that starry night had the same name as my father.

At that moment, the intensity of the evening rose, and my mind drifted between anxiety and curiosity.

It was then, amidst that whirlwind of sensation, that Jorge, with his characteristic joy, exclaimed:

—*"I have an idea! Will you marry me?"*

What a beautiful phrase.

I extended my DIY manicured hand and replied:

—*"What a great idea!"*

However, the migraine never went away —as a warning that marrying him might bring along many headaches…

CHAPTER NINE
THANK YOU THREE TIMES

If the life you have isn't the life you want, it's very likely your thoughts have a lot to do with it. Or maybe, everything to do with it. Let me explain. Our reality is the direct result of our thoughts. It's an invisible yet powerful chain: what you think generates an emotion, that emotion emits a frequency, that frequency influences your actions, and your actions create your results. If the results you're seeing don't please you, it's time to examine your thoughts.

I remember perfectly one Saturday morning in September, while I was getting ready to give the final live class of my "Letter to the Universe" course. The theme that day was none other than **"gratitude."** As I was about to begin, my daughter Victoria dropped a bombshell: her dad would come to my youngest son's birthday… with his new wife. A woman I had never met in person.

I almost canceled the class. I felt a knot in my chest, my breathing accelerated, and my thoughts overflowed like a wave of judgment and rage. "What's wrong with him? How dare he come here with her? Without warning? I'm going to kill him!" My mind, as a good dramatic storyteller, took me straight to the edge. I was seconds from acting impulsively… but the clock reminded me I had a live class. My students were waiting. I took a breath. I sat in front of the camera and started the broadcast, even though my mind and heart were still swirling.

I decided to be honest. "Life is very funny," I told them. "The universe knows what it's doing, even when we don't like it. Today I have to teach you a class on gratitude… and the last thing I feel right now is gratitude." I told them what was happening, and in telling it, something began to shift in me. As if simply voicing it, acknowledging it out loud, allowed me to observe the situation from another angle.

That's when I understood: this lesson wasn't only for them. It was for me. Because giving a class on gratitude is easy when everything flows, when there's health, food on the table, love, and life seems on track. But the real challenge, the true mastery, lies in giving thanks when all you want is to shout or run. When you feel hurt, uncomfortable, challenged.

I shared a tool that in that moment I started to apply in real time: the "Thank-You-Thrice" method. A practice that has changed my life and that I share with you now so you can make it your own:

1. **First, be grateful for the past.** Honor what you've lived through, even the hard parts. Gratitude for the past sets you free.
   - I took a deep breath and gave thanks for all the times I had felt pain in that relationship, because thanks to that, today I have awareness, growth, and evolution.
2. **Then, give thanks for the present.** For what is in front of you, even if it's not perfect. Even if it's uncomfortable.
   - I was grateful that if I was going to meet my ex's wife, it would be here, in my space, with my people, at a children's party where I felt supported. I was grateful I could observe her without judgment. I was grateful to feel strong, confident, and centered.
3. **And finally, give thanks for the future.** For what hasn't happened yet, but you are already ready to receive.

- I visualized myself in peace. I saw myself beyond that encounter. I imagined myself free, living my best version. And I gave thanks in advance—for the woman I am becoming, for the mother I am, and for the life I am creating.

And so, with that renewed energy, with that shift in perception—which is itself a miracle—I transformed. I remembered what *A Course in Miracles* teaches: when you can't see something with love, ask for help to change your perception. The course teaches that when you can't see a situation positively, you ask the Holy Spirit to show it to you differently. **The shift in perception *is* the miracle.**

I also recalled a tool from Kabbalah that I love: when something makes you uncomfortable or pulls you out of your center, pause, breathe, and say: **"What a pleasure, what an opportunity."** Not sarcastically, but as an affirmation that *this too* has a purpose. What we're trying to do here is see the challenge as a growth opportunity—a moment to pass a test that leads to your highest good. These tests come so you can shift beliefs, face traumas, and heal wounds.

And that's how it was. I got it. This situation didn't come to ruin my day, but to show me how strong I've become. To give me a chance to practice what I preach. To live from my authenticity.

In that moment, I connected with my essence. I told myself, **"I won't act from ego or from pain. I'll act from my power."** And when it came time for us to meet, I greeted her with a kiss, looked her in the eyes, invited her in, and treated her as I would any guest. Not pretending, but with respect. Not with hypocrisy, but with love. I was myself. I was that version of me that has taken so much to build.

And at the end of the day, it was a beautiful party. It was the best class I've ever given. And it was also a divine gift. Because gratitude is one of the most powerful energies there is. It doesn't transform situations—but it transforms how we experience them. It raises our frequency. It opens new doors. It brings us back to the present.

And when you give thanks three times—for what was, for what is, and for what will be—something inside you rearranges. You align. And what seemed like a storm becomes light.

The shift in perception *is* the miracle.

Pause.

What a pleasure.

Thank you. Thank you. Thank you.

CHAPTER TEN
MAKE SHIFT HAPPEN

After two years as a hotel manager, when I finally had an apparently stable life—a house in my name, the car paid off, the divorce finalized, my green card in hand, my children settling in—I found myself at a new crossroads. Everything looked good on paper. Anyone would say, "You've made it." But something inside me asked, "Then what? Is this where the story ends?"

The truth is, I knew it wasn't. My soul was restless, my heart alight with a certainty that came not from logic: this wasn't my happy ending... it was the beginning.

I decided to resign. Just like that, with no Plan B. And when I told my boss I was leaving, he looked at me with a mixture of confusion and a hint of disappointment. He said bluntly, "This is the dumbest thing I've ever heard." And I don't blame him. Who in their right mind resigns from a stable salary as a single mom of three in the U.S., with a mortgage and no other job lined up? Well... me.

Because I don't follow conventional formulas. I listen to my soul. And my soul asked me to leap.

I left with fear, of course. Real fear. The kind that tightens your chest and gives you nausea. But I also left with hope, with the vibrational certainty that if this leap was guided by love—not by fear... the universe would support me. And I only take orders from God.

And yes: **Make Shift Happen.**

A few weeks later, I received news that confirmed it all. There was a firm offer to buy my lot in Mexico—the land I'd purchased with hard-earned commissions and couldn't sell because of the country's oil crisis. Boom! Unexpected income that gave me breathing room, covered my expenses, and allowed me to support my children without rushing to find another job. That money arrived as a vibrational reward—a gentle pat from the universe saying, *"You're on the right path. Keep going."*

I began to move. To create. To show up. To share what I knew and what I was experiencing. I jumped in with no safety net, with more truth than structure, more heart than strategy.

It was then that I reconnected with Julie, a friend from Barranquilla whom I'd reached out to again during the pandemic. Our stories seemed cut from the same cloth—divorced, moms of three, die-hard dreamers, obsessed with personal development, and driven by the urgent need to share what we were learning amid our own transformations. During lockdown we exchanged messages, reflections, supported each other at a distance... but something inside me whispered that we needed to do more.

The idea had been buzzing in my mind for a while. One night, after a long call—one of those conversations where every mask falls—I proposed: *"What if we do a podcast?"*

She responded without hesitation: *"Let's do it!"*

And that's how Sanando Ando (I Am Healing) was born.

We started recording with what we had: a Zoom, one story, and a thousand desires. We did it whenever our schedules aligned. Some-

IT'S NOT MAGIC; IT'S FREQUENCY

times half-asleep, sometimes with hoarse voices, but always with open hearts. It was our safe space. Our release valve. Our trench of love and truth.

Sanando Ando Podcast became our refuge to talk about everything that connected us: the mind, relationships, health, attachment styles, masculine and feminine energies, astrology, mindset, spirituality.

From that also sprang **Sanando Ando Club**, a living, vibrant community that grew week by week. And with every session we held, it became clearer to me: **this is my purpose. This is me.**

Supporting processes, holding space, offering tools based on lived experience, not just what's been read.

And the most powerful thing: every time I supported someone in their process, *I* healed too.

The Law of Correspondence activated. Energy doesn't lie. What you give, you receive multiplied.

Amid that personal boom, **Latina Empire** appeared—a community of women who work on their hearts, minds, and money all at once. More kindred minds…

It's like when you see one ant, and suddenly there's an army: *they multiply!*

I became one of their global leaders, and everything took on even more power.

I was no longer just Carolina—the coach or the author. I was part of something bigger. **A movement. A transformation network.**

It was also during that period that I met **Giselle, Eliza, Esther, Magdalena, Aileen, and Marie**—women who would become not just friends, but **Mastermind sisters**: an alliance of purpose where we support each other, elevate each other, and empower one another to grow in every area of life.

. . .

That's when I understood why life had taken me to McAllen. It wasn't because of Jorge. It wasn't because of the divorce.

It was to be reborn in the midst of chaos. It was to remember that even in the most unexpected place, you can bloom. God had another plan. A better one.

And the more I surrendered to service, the clearer the vision became.

It was no longer a vague idea. It was a luminous certainty: to open paths in the world of personal development for the Hispanic market.

To create transformative books. To share inspiring conferences. To support emotional and energetic healing processes. To found living communities. To be a guide, a present mother, a voice and soul in motion. To impact millions of lives: that became the North Star.

Shifting the energy of a space became a conscious gift.

In some way, it had always been that way.

In Barranquilla, as a child, when my friends' spirits were down, all it took was a "¡Saca saca, baby!" to get us moving, to release sadness to the frenzied rhythm of mapalé.

Years later, that would give birth to **Saca Saca Therapy Dance**: a vibrational practice that feels like play, but is healing in motion.

Because the body stores what the mind doesn't know how to process.

And when you move with intention, you release.

And when you release, you make space.

And when you make space, you receive.

That is the formula:

You release what holds you back.

You receive what expands you and you embody it with your whole being.

. . .

Today I understand that energy isn't just another item on the priority list. It's everything. It's the root. The filter. The language through which the universe responds to us. It's not about being happy all the time or living in perpetual bliss. It's about returning to yourself every time you get lost. About having the courage to sit with yourself, with your light and your shadows, without rushing, without judgment, with love.

Because the true shift isn't always an explosion. Sometimes it's a whisper. Sometimes it's a silence that feels like home. Sometimes it's a surrender, an "I can't take this anymore" that turns into an "I finally understand."

Transformation isn't always shouted. Many times, it's cried quietly, honored in private, sustained in the everyday. Changing your energy doesn't mean stopping yourself from feeling—it means allowing yourself to feel everything… without getting lost in the chaos. It's learning to observe without reacting, to pause without giving up, to hold yourself without hardening.

And when you learn to live this way, you start truly living. Not from autopilot, but from awareness. Not from survival, but from creation.

That's when life starts speaking to you differently. It opens doors you didn't even know existed. It returns parts of yourself you thought were lost. It shows you that you weren't broken—you were simply remembering your power.

So if something stirs within you as you read these words, don't ignore it. Listen to yourself. You don't need to do it all today. You just need to begin. One step. One breath. One decision.

And when you do it, when you choose yourself from truth and not from fear, when you release control and embrace your highest frequency… then yes:

Get ready.

Because the universe doesn't respond to your words.

It responds to your frequency.

And there, right there, is where the magic happens.

CHAPTER ELEVEN
ALIGNED ACTION

If thoughts generate emotions and those emotions, in turn, generate actions, make sure your actions align with your positive thoughts—those that reflect your vision.

During my teenage years and even until a few years ago, my actions were impulsive.

I would let myself be entirely led by my emotions, which resulted in extreme decisions from one day to the next, because my emotions and hormones changed daily.

It was an incredible instability that sometimes worked—but other times, definitely didn't.

The common denominator was action; people used to say:

"This woman is a force to be reckoned with!"

When I got an idea, I would immediately start researching and taking action.

It didn't matter how big the effort or the investment: if something got into my head, there was no way to convince me otherwise.

For me, nothing was impossible.

That's how I opened and closed businesses, organized parties and trips —always guided by my impulses, which I often called intuition, although they didn't always come from that place.

Many times, those impulses came from scarcity (low frequency); others, from abundance (high frequency)—and that's where the results showed whether they worked or not.

When I finished high school in Barranquilla, I was at a crossroads: I didn't know exactly what I wanted to study.

I had two options: move to Bogotá with my grandfather and study Social Communication, with the idea of becoming an actress—taking advantage of the fact that he had many contacts in that industry and was friends with Fanny Mikey, the director of the Teatro Nacional and his island neighbor in the Islas del Rosario—

Or move to Austin, Texas, with my grandmother Mami Ann, who lived there, and where the University of Texas at Austin had a great reputation.

I don't remember why I decided to go to Austin instead of Bogotá, but the truth is, I hadn't been accepted into that university.

So my first few months were spent in an intensive English institute (a language I already mastered), simply waiting while I applied to the university and took the corresponding admission tests.

Four months passed, I applied, and I received a rejection letter.

I hadn't been accepted to UT Austin due to my SAT scores.

I couldn't stay another semester wasting time in the English academy, so my dad said to me:

"You'll have to come back to Barranquilla."

To me, that felt like punishment; I was making a lot of friends in Austin, and seeing the UT campus had made leaving no longer an option.

So I decided to look for unconventional ways to get in.

I wrote an email to the communications department titled "Another Sheep in the Flock."

In the message, I explained that I was Colombian, that I had come to Austin to study, and that I wanted to know what my options were for getting into the university, since my dream was to study advertising.

Surprisingly, I received a response that filled me with hope.

They told me the head of that department was Dean Quinn, the dean of the School of Communications.

I had a name!

Hope was still alive, so I ran out to find him.

I arrived at the School of Communications offices and asked for an appointment with him.

The receptionist told me she was very sorry, but the offices were already closed for the semester; she said I should request an appointment for the next semester, which would begin after the winter break.

To me, that was serious; if I went to Barranquilla for Christmas without being accepted, they wouldn't let me come back.

That burning desire was still alive, and as I was walking toward the exit, I saw a nameplate on an office door: Dean Quinn. The door was slightly open, I peeked in, and there he was.

"Come in," he said. "Come on in!"

I couldn't believe what was happening. I had the dean right in front of me, and I needed to make my pitch short and powerful.

"How can I help you?" he asked.

I told him I was Colombian, that I had come to Austin because my grandmother lived there, that my dream was to study at this university, and that I hadn't done well on the math portion of the SAT, which was why I had been rejected.

But I made it clear to him that I knew I didn't need to be a math expert for advertising, that I was an excellent communicator, and that I was fully committed to giving it my all.

I also told him that if I went to Barranquilla for the winter break without being accepted, they wouldn't let me come back.

And who knows how many more things I told that poor man.

With a gentle and inspiring look, he replied:

"You're a persistent, dream-driven young woman, and with this positive mindset and determination to succeed, you're going to go very far. Give me your full name and expect a letter in the mail. Happy holidays!"

And that's how my acceptance letter to UT Austin arrived—through the most unconventional path possible.

Thanks to my action aligned with my vision, I was able to turn a "no" into a "yes" through a torrent of persuasion and courage.

Looking back, I realize that experience was more than just a university admission process; it was a true testament that when we follow our intuition and our passion, and when we are bold enough to take initiative, we can open doors where there were once only walls.

So there I was, about to begin a new adventure at a university I had longed for.

More importantly, I was ready to embrace that part of me that had been tucked away—full of creativity, dreams, and the firm belief that I could do what I truly desired.

It's not magic, it's frequency.

But how do you know if the decision (followed by action) you're about to make is aligned or well-aspected?

It's taken me half a lifetime and countless failures to understand this principle:

If what I'm about to do or say supports the life I want, I proceed.

Your vision.

Action aligned with your vision.

Imagine the life of your dreams and then look at what part of that life you're already living.

Is it all very far away?

Are you on the right path?

What's missing for you to get there?

If the life you have (your results) is not close to the life you want (your vision), then you're making the wrong decisions.

Does the future version of your ideal life practice the habits you currently have?

Drive the car you're driving now?

Dress the way you dress at this moment?

Do what you currently do for a living?

If your answer to any of these questions is no, then it's clear you're not acting like your future self or your best version.

Small actions create big differences; that's where everything changes.

Remember, the key is to take aligned action.

That means acting when you truly feel the decision resonates with you.

It's not just about doing for the sake of doing; it's about making sure each action points toward your goals and aspirations.

By adopting a mindset of growth and aligned action, you don't just begin to transform your life, you also lay the foundation to attract the experiences you truly desire.

Do you remember the car my stepfather gave me?

The used 2016 Kia Sorento.

At that time, the future version of Carolina needed a job to survive (at the hotel), and that car was a perfect fit.

I still felt vulnerable and had a scarcity mindset.

The car was perfect! More than I needed, and free.

Wow! I was blessed and chosen by God.

Over the years, after quitting and with a higher sense of self-worth, I dedicated myself to my life's purpose.

I got certified as a Coach from the Napoleon Hill Institute and became one of the top ten coaches in the Hispanic market, giving conferences and doing everything I had dreamed of...

But I was still driving the same 2016 Kia Sorento.

One day, during a trip to San Antonio, Texas, my daughter Victoria pointed out a car passing by and said:

"That's the car I want when I grow up—a white BMW X5."

I was stunned; how amazing that she knew exactly the color, brand, and model of the car she wanted!

I looked at my little Kia, and during the drive back to McAllen, my mind couldn't stop thinking about the white BMW X5 that Victoria liked.

I asked myself:

Does the car I drive represent the future version of Carolina, the one who impacts thousands of people with her books, conferences, and courses?

That Carolina would drive a current model BMW, not an old model Kia.

When I got home, I searched online:

"White BMW X5 McAllen"

And—boom!—a semi-new one popped up.

The truth was, I didn't have extra money to buy a new car, but since manifesting the "how" isn't my problem, I went to sleep leaving the task to my subconscious.

Before bed, I visualized the car, saw myself in it, and told it:

"Find a way for that car to be mine."

That was it.

I gave my subconscious a job to do—one that works 24/7 to find solutions to the instructions I give it.

But I couldn't just leave it at that, without taking aligned action with my vision.

So the next morning, I got up early (a habit of future Carolina), joined my 5 a.m. call with my Mastermind group, went to the gym, and when I got back, I got ready to start my client calls.

In the middle of that, a client cancels!

Hmm, okay.

I'll get all dressed up—super fabulous—and go see the car at the BMW dealership.

I got ready like the future Carolina who drives that car, picked up my friend Maryfer—who always hypes me up—and told her:

"Let's go get my new car."

Without hesitation, she hopped into my Kia and off we went.

She just looked at me and said:

"I love it! I love it!"

We arrived at the BMW dealership with triumphant energy; both of us were radiating contagious vibes.

When we got there, the excitement was in the air.

We test-drove the white BMW X5, and in that moment, I felt like my best self.

Then we started reviewing financing options to see if I'd be approved for a loan.

As a solopreneur running my small coaching business, I wasn't sure if I'd qualify for the credit I needed, and I had no idea what my monthly payment would be.

Maybe I'd need to trade in the Kia as part of the deal, but none of that kept me up at night.

While they were reviewing the financials, I get a video call from my mom.

"Caro, my financial advisor just called me about my stocks, and he said he's going to send me a check for $18,000 from a return on an investment.

I'm going to send it to you because I recently sent the same amount to your brother for a business venture, so I owe it to you to keep things even—as a living inheritance.

I'll transfer it to you now."

WHAAAT???

I nearly fainted.

My friend and the dealership manager, who were both listening to the call, were just as stunned as I was.

Now I had more than enough for the down payment and to move forward with the purchase—without even needing to trade in the Kia.

I left the dealership with the new car, ready to pick up my kids from school and eager to see Victoria's face when she realized that every dream can come true...

As long as we have clarity about what we want and what we deserve.

It was an instant manifestation;

gratitude rushed through my veins,

reaffirming again and again that it's not magic—it's frequency!

CHAPTER TWELVE

THE UNIVERSE OBEYS

During my years of marriage, I tried to control so many things. From small decisions to truly significant matters: how to interact with his family, which activities were appropriate, how we should raise our children. I even thought I could persuade him to stay away from politics. I was frustrated that he didn't act the way I wanted. That he didn't understand my emotions the way I needed. That he didn't react the way I expected.

My upbringing had been different. We were two worlds trying to coexist under the same roof. We communicated logically, but we related from different wounds. We assumed too much, spoke too little, and communicated deeply even less. No one taught us that before getting married, you need to talk about everything: values, boundaries, extended family, parenting styles, what is negotiable and what is not. And so, with no map or manual, we got lost in the attempt.

I tried to impose what I believed was right. And he, of course, resisted. We entered a toxic cycle of assumptions, blame, and disagreements. The more I felt I didn't have control, the harder I tried to get it. The more I pushed my point of view. What I was really trying to avoid was feeling rejected, invisible, unheard.

And since everything is energy, that constant struggle lowered my frequency. My thoughts were destructive: "This isn't working," "we're not compatible," "maybe we should separate." Phrases I threw into the air from my frustration, from the wound, but said with emotion. And when you speak with emotion, you're manifesting. You're ordering the universe to return exactly what you feel.

Recently, Jorge confessed something that shook me:

—From how much you told me this wasn't working, I ended up believing it.

That's when I understood the absolute power of words when they're repeated, felt, decreed with conviction. What one believes, one creates. And, unknowingly, I had begun manifesting the divorce long before it happened.

I'm not saying it was all my fault. Relationships don't end because of just one person. But I do take responsibility for the role I played, the emotions I couldn't manage, the words I let out without understanding their impact.

Control was my mask. But behind the control, there was fear. And fear is the opposite of faith. When you try to control, you are not trusting. And if you don't trust, you don't flow. You're blocking everything: energy, love, abundance, expansion.

The tension grew. Inside I felt broken, confused, stuck. Each day was an emotional drain. Until one day, everything collapsed. I sank into a deep depression. I gave myself completely to external factors. To other people's opinions. To diagnoses. To pills.

I allowed a psychiatrist to prescribe me such strong medication that, during a family vacation, I had to request a wheelchair to get around an amusement park because I simply couldn't walk properly. I was disconnected from myself. From my body. From my power.

I became a drifter. Just as Napoleon Hill describes in *Outwitting the Devil*: a person who doesn't think for themselves and hands their life over to circumstances, to what others say, to what the system dictates.

But in the midst of that emptiness, something awakened in me. An inner voice, a deep intuition, shouted clearly:

"No one has power over you. And you don't have power over anyone. Let go of the damn control."

And I let it go.

I threw away the pills. I went to the sea. I dipped my feet in the water with the intention that the salt would cleanse my energy. I dyed my hair. I got my nails done. I sipped a coffee slowly. I hugged my kids. My dog. I turned on the radio. I let music fill the house. I sat down to write.

And something inside me began to realign. Little by little, my energy shifted. And since everything is frequency, the circumstances also began to change. It wasn't magic.

With that new frequency, I understood something much greater: **words are spells.**

It's not about thinking pretty thoughts or repeating empty affirmations. It's about speaking from the truth of your soul. Because every word you say is an energetic command. A code. An order. And the universe always obeys.

We've been made to believe that spells only exist in fairy tales. But no. Spells are cast every day. They're called words.

Each *"this is too much for me"*, *"I can't take it anymore"*, *"nothing ever goes right for me"*, *"the same thing always happens to me"*... are disguised decrees. And life doesn't punish. Life obeys.

I experienced it with my dad. He died of leukemia. But the most shocking part wasn't his death, it was his anticipation of it. Ten years earlier, his fingers started turning purple. Poor circulation, they said. He began taking blood thinners. I was ten. He was forty. One day, scared, I asked him if he was going to die. He calmly replied:

—*No, I still have ten more years to live.*

And so it was. Exactly ten years later, his body gave in.

He declared it. He said it. He believed it. He manifested it.

That memory, which I had stored away for years without understanding, now takes on new meaning. His phrase was a spell. An energetic pact. An affirmation so powerful that his body aligned with it.

Today, I'm aware that every time I speak about myself, my life, my dreams, my body, my health, or my future… I'm creating. That's why I do it with more intention. With more care. With more respect for that invisible power we all have.

My marriage ended, yes. But my life was just beginning. Because in that separation, I found my freedom, my identity, my strength. I'm grateful it happened the way it did. Because thanks to that, I was able to recover what I had most lost: myself.

THE CIRCLE CLOSES

It's been five years since the day my world shattered.

Five years since I crossed a border with my heart in my hands and four suitcases full of uncertainty.

Five years of rebuilding myself piece by piece, of emptying out so I could fill back up, of remembering who I was… and who I was always meant to be.

Today, the circle closes.

I've become a U.S. citizen.

I've listed the house that held me while I healed.

And I've launched this book — a testimony, an offering, a rebirth.

My soul, once convinced it had no home, now whispers softly but surely: *"It's time to go back."*

Barranquilla is calling.

My people, my family, my roots.

One cycle ends… and a new one begins.

I don't know what awaits me on the other side, but this time, I'm not running. I'm choosing.

Not from pain, but from wholeness.

Not searching for shelter, but ready to expand.

And who knows…

maybe life still has one more "wow" in store for me.

The kind you never see coming — but always feel in your soul.

FINAL WORDS

This is what I want you to take from this story:

The universe isn't punishing or rewarding you. The universe obeys. Always.

If you vibrate from fear, you'll attract more fear. If you vibrate from lack, more lack.

But if you vibrate from gratitude, from certainty, from worthiness… then you'll open the doors to a completely different reality.

Life doesn't change when you control everything. It changes when you let go, raise your frequency, and trust. Because that's when the real magic happens: not when you force it, but when you allow it.

The universe doesn't question. It doesn't doubt. It only responds.

And if you change your frequency, your experience will inevitably change.

Life doesn't give you what you wish for. **It gives you what you vibrate.**

When you raise your internal standard, the universe responds effortlessly.

When you stop asking for permission to dream, and act like the one who's already achieved it, miracles stop being exceptions… **and become your new normal.**

"Frequency isn't a destination. It's the path. And your energy... is the language the universe never stops listening to."

I wish for the magic in your life to be permanent, and for that magic to be the reflection of your highest frequency.

With all my love and the best of my vibes,

Caro.

TOOL KIT

I hope my story has inspired you and that you've found tools you can apply to your own life.

That's why, in the following pages, you'll find the **Toolkit:** a compilation of the practices, exercises, and principles that have accompanied me on this path of transformation.

Practical resources to raise your frequency and manifest consciously.

This kit isn't just an appendix. It's an energetic training ground.

A living guide to help you remember what you already know: frequency isn't a concept… it's the solution.

Everything you're experiencing has a vibrational root.

Your external reality is a mirror of your internal frequency.

And the best part is that you can change it. You can move up a level. You can redirect your energy.

Here you'll find tools to:

- Reconnect with yourself
- Raise your vibrational frequency
- Align your energy with what you desire
- Activate manifestations from a place of consciousness

THE 5R METHOD OF MANIFESTATION

Five inner movements to transform your frequency... and your reality.

This channeled and lived method guides you step by step through the energetic process of conscious manifestation.

Each R represents an emotional and vibrational stage that prepares you to receive what you desire—without forcing, without controlling, and without self-deception.

~

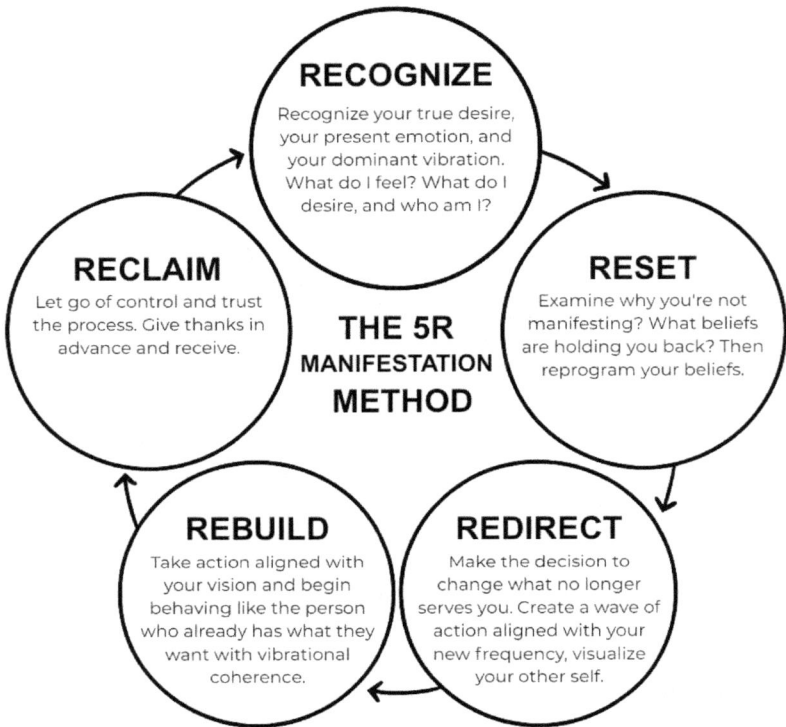

RECOGNIZE
Recognize your true desire, your present emotion, and your dominant vibration. What do I feel? What do I desire, and who am I?

RESET
Examine why you're not manifesting? What beliefs are holding you back? Then reprogram your beliefs.

RECLAIM
Let go of control and trust the process. Give thanks in advance and receive.

THE 5R MANIFESTATION METHOD

REDIRECT
Make the decision to change what no longer serves you. Create a wave of action aligned with your new frequency, visualize your other self.

REBUILD
Take action aligned with your vision and begin behaving like the person who already has what they want with vibrational coherence.

RECOGNIZE

What do I want? Who am I really?

Recognize is the first step. It's about honestly looking at where you are and what you want to create from authenticity—not from what others expect.

Here, you connect with your true desire, not a borrowed one.

Example: I don't just want a job; I want purpose. I don't just want a partner; I want real emotional connection.

Energetic keys:

- Observe your truth without judgment
- Define your non-negotiable values
- Admit what you no longer want
- Visualize the life you do want

Practical example – When a project gets canceled:

RECOGNIZE: I feel frustrated, disappointed, and afraid. I recognize that this project represented hope and validation. I also acknowledge that I am feeding thoughts of failure and scarcity.

~

RESET

What beliefs are holding me back? What story am I telling myself?

This step is like clearing the soil before planting. Here, you release the beliefs that anchor you to past versions of yourself. You reprogram your mind and your emotional system.

Example: "I'll never be able to do it alone" → "I'm learning to support myself from my inner power."

Energetic keys:

- Identify inherited limiting beliefs
- Use affirmations as antidotes
- Forgive your past story
- Observe your thoughts with awareness

Practical example (continued):

RESET: This situation does not define my worth. I release the belief that if something falls through, it's because I'm not enough. I rewrite the story: "This project didn't choose me because something better is on its way."

∼

REDIRECT

Where do I want to go and how do I want to feel?

This step is energetic. There's no external action yet, but you're already planting elevated emotion. Here, you activate visualization, clear intention, and vibrational preparation.

Example: Create a vision board. Write your letter to the universe. Sit in silence and visualize your future as if it's already real.

Energetic keys:

- Elevate your emotion before taking action
- Visualize from a place of certainty
- Create energetic structure: give thanks, meditate, declare
- Plant with intention

Practical example (continued):

REDIRECT: I visualize new doors opening. I feel in my body the energy of a more aligned opportunity. I write in my journal: "I'm ready to receive something that expands me even more."

∼

REBUILD

How does my best version act?

It's time to align your behavior with your new identity. You're not pretending. You're embodying. You walk like someone who has already achieved it.

Example: You act with confidence in an interview because you're no longer begging for validation; you're offering value from your authenticity.

Energetic keys:

- Make decisions from expansion
- Live as if you're already there
- Speak, dress, walk like your highest self
- You don't wait to become—you become

Practical example (continued):

REBUILD: Instead of freezing, I update my portfolio, reconnect with contacts, and send a message with my new proposal. I act from my best version, not from the wound.

∼

RECLAIM

Am I willing to receive without controlling the how?

This is where you let go. This is where you trust. This is where you allow. The energy has already been planted; now you open yourself to receive with certainty.

Example: Instead of chasing answers, you trust in perfect timing. Instead of doubting, you give thanks in advance.

Energetic keys:

- Let go of obsession with the outcome
- Trust your frequency
- Live like someone who already has it
- Give thanks from the future

Practical example (conclusion):

RECLAIM: I relax. I trust. I give thanks for what's coming even if it hasn't yet manifested. I know that if something fell apart, it's because something more vibrationally aligned is waiting for me.

. . .

Long-term Application Example – Expansive Vision:

RECOGNIZE: I desire a life of global impact, free time, financial freedom, vibrant health, a loving relationship, travel with my kids, and a community that grows with my message.

RESET: I let go of the belief that I must sacrifice my well-being for success. That "you can't have it all." I reprogram with the belief: "I deserve a full life in every area."

REDIRECT: I write a letter to the universe. I visualize my ideal days. I create a vision board. I feel that life as if it's already real. I vibrate in expansion, joy, certainty.

REBUILD: I make decisions aligned with that vision. I invest in education, heal my relationships, take care of my body, design my services.

RECLAIM: I live in anticipatory gratitude. I open myself to receive without control. I trust divine timing and enjoy the process. It's all already happening.

Integration Phrase: **"It doesn't manifest when you need it. It manifests when you're vibrating at the same frequency as what you desire."**

The Energetic Path to Your New Reality

This method is not a theory: it is a deep vibrational practice. It helps you manifest from the root — not through effort, but through energetic coherence.

You can apply it to:

✔ Make big or daily decisions
✔ Accelerate deep transformation
✔ Return to yourself when you feel lost
✔ Create with clarity from your authenticity

The 5Rs:

Steps	Key Question	Energy Action
RECOGNIZE	Where am I really and what do I want?	Observe your truth without judgment. Find the source.
RESET	What story am I telling myself?	Question, let go, and rewrite your narrative.
REDIRECT	What actions can I take from my new energy?	Visualize. Declare. Sow emotion.
REBUILD	How does my elevated version behave?	Act consistently. Embody your vision.
RECLAIM	Am I open to receiving without controlling how?	Let go. Trust. Open your arms.

Affirmations by R:

- **RECOGNIZE**: I acknowledge myself with love, unafraid of my truth.
- **RESET**: I am reprogramming my mind to receive miracles.
- **REDIRECT**: I take action from certainty, not from lack.
- **REBUILD**: I already am who my soul came here to be.
- **RECLAIM**: I am ready to receive what is mine by divine right.

Integration Phrase: An aligned mind creates an aligned reality.

LAWS OF THE UNIVERSE

These laws are not commandments or rigid rules. They are energetic principles that govern the universe. By integrating them into your daily life, you begin to manifest with more ease, clarity, and purpose.

Universal laws do not judge, they only **respond to your vibration.**

When you understand them and apply them… everything begins to align.

~

1. LAW OF VIBRATION

Everything vibrates. So do you.

- **Meaning:** Everything in the universe is in motion. Every thought, emotion, and word emits a frequency.
- **Practice:** Before taking action, ask yourself: From what frequency am I vibrating? If it's fear or doubt, shift: breathe, dance, declare an affirmation.
- **Example:** You're about to send an important message. Do it from confidence, not anxiety. Your energy is transmitted.

2. LAW OF ATTRACTION

You don't attract what you desire; you attract what you are.

- **Meaning:** The universe responds to your frequency, not your words.
- **Practice:** Feel as if you already have it. Act from certainty. Ask yourself: What would my most abundant self do today?
- **Example:** If you want love, treat yourself with love. You are the first magnet.

3. LAW OF CORRESPONDENCE

As within, so without.

- **Meaning:** Your external world reflects your internal state.
- **Practice:** Observe your surroundings. What part of you is being reflected in that?
- **Example:** If you constantly feel rejected, maybe there's something within you that you still haven't accepted.

4. LAW OF RHYTHM

Everything flows and ebbs.

- **Meaning:** Life moves in cycles. Nothing is permanent.
- **Practice:** Honor your rhythm. Rest when your body asks for it. Accelerate when your energy allows it.
- **Example:** Don't blame yourself for being in pause. It's part of the balance.

5. LAW OF CAUSE AND EFFECT

Everything you give, comes back.

- **Meaning:** Every action generates a reaction, whether energetic or material.
- **Practice:** Give from the heart, without expectation.
- **Example:** You help someone with love. Days later, an unexpected opportunity opens up. Nothing is a coincidence.

6. LAW OF POLARITY

Everything has its opposite.

- **Meaning:** Light and shadow coexist. One gives meaning to the other.
- **Practice:** When something hurts, remember: this too shall pass. Look for the lesson behind it.
- **Example:** Losing a job can be the doorway to your true calling.

7. LAW OF GENDER

Balance between the feminine and the masculine.

- **Meaning:** We all have feminine energy (intuitive) and masculine energy (active). Harmony happens when they are balanced.
- **Practice:** If you're exhausted, activate your receptive side. If you're feeling stuck, take action from your executive side.
- **Example:** If you're waiting without acting, you need structure. If you're acting non-stop, you need a pause.

Law	Essential Message	Practical Example
Vibration	Everything vibrates. Your energy emits a frequency.	Breathe before you act. Vibrate from calm.
Attraction	You attract what you are, not what you desire.	Be the love you want to receive.
Correspondence	As it is within, so it is without.	Your environment reflects your internal state.
Rhythm	Everything has cycles. Honor your timing.	Don't blame yourself for pausing. It's part of the process.
Cause and Effect	What you give, comes back.	Give from the heart, without expectations.
Polarity	Everything has its opposite.	Every shadow brings a lesson of light.
Gender	Female and male energy balances.	If you're exhausted, receive. If you're stuck, act.

The laws are neither punishment nor reward. They are responses to your frequency.

Apply them with awareness. And watch how the universe, little by little, begins to respond to your new frequency.

LETTER TO THE UNIVERSE

What's it for?

The Letter to the Universe is a vibrational tool that allows you to manifest with clarity, intention, and faith. It is a symbolic and energetic act where you declare what you desire from your most authentic self. This letter **is not for asking from a place of lack**, but for expressing gratitude, visualizing, and releasing your desires with trust.

It's for:

- Clarifying your true desires
- Connecting with the frequency of gratitude and possibility
- Visualizing your new reality from the present
- Raising your energy and strengthen your faith
- Letting go of control and surrender to the universe with certainty

A powerful practice to activate your quantum field

The Letter to the Universe is a vibrational tool to declare your desires with clarity, gratitude, and certainty. You don't ask from lack. You give thanks as if it were already real.

How to write it?

1. **Greet with intention**
   - Use whatever resonates most with you: "Dear Universe," "Dear Life," "My Higher Self," etc.
2. **Give thanks for what you already have**
   - Gratitude raises your frequency.
3. **State your desires with clarity**
   - Use the present tense: "I am grateful for…", "I live in…", "I enjoy…"
4. **Visualize as you write**
   - Connect with the emotion. Write it as if you were already living it.
5. **Close with certainty and surrender**
   - Phrases like: "Thank you, thank you, thank you. And so it is. It's already mine."
6. **Sign with your name**
   - Seal your intention with your energy.

Final recommendation:

Keep your letter in a special place or burn it as a symbolic act of surrender. You can repeat this exercise with each new moon, at the end of a cycle, or whenever you need to reconnect with your vision.

Activation phrase:

"And so it is. It's already mine. Thank you, thank you, thank you."

VIBRATIONAL FREQUENCIES

The Building of Your Energy: Every Emotion Takes You to a Different Floor

Imagine your life as a building.

Each emotion you vibrate in takes you to a different level.

The higher the frequency, the more light, vision, and expansion.

The lower it is, the more darkness, more confusion, more heaviness.

The basement is where emotions like shame (20), guilt (30), apathy (50), or fear (100) reside. It's dark, dense, full of mental cockroaches and emotional dampness. Your mirror doesn't even want to look at you.

The penthouse, on the other hand, is the space where peace (600), love (500), joy (540), or enlightenment (700+) reside. There's light, abundance, fresh air, beautiful views, and even your own vibrational chef.

Between both extremes, there are many intermediate floors. And most importantly: **you can move between them.** You're not trapped.

🎬 **And how do you go up?**

With intention. With practice.

But above all… with gratitude.

Gratitude is the elevator button.

∾

FREQUENCY OF EMOTIONS

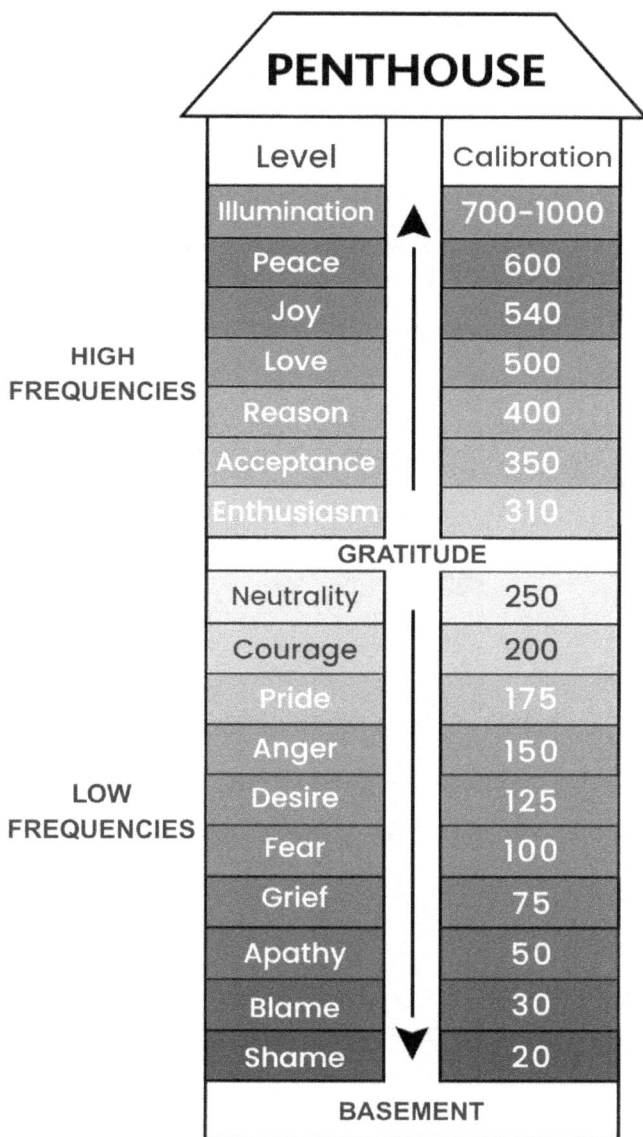

PENTHOUSE

Level	Calibration
Illumination	700–1000
Peace	600
Joy	540
Love	500
Reason	400
Acceptance	350
Enthusiasm	310

HIGH FREQUENCIES

GRATITUDE

Level	Calibration
Neutrality	250
Courage	200
Pride	175
Anger	150
Desire	125
Fear	100
Grief	75
Apathy	50
Blame	30
Shame	20

LOW FREQUENCIES

BASEMENT

🔍 EXAMPLES OF FREQUENCY ACCORDING TO EMOTION

Floor	Emotion	Frequency	How it feels
Penthouse	Illumination	700–1000	Total fullness, divine connection.
	Peace	600	Serenity, unity, clarity.
	Joy	540	Calm euphoria, joy, expansion.
	Love	500	Self-love, empathy, total acceptance.
	Reason	400	Mental clarity, objectivity, focus.
	Acceptance	350	Surrender without resignation.
	Enthusiasm	310	Motivation, positive energy.
GRATITUDE	Gratitude	—	The bridge. The energy that lifts you up.
Transition	Neutrality	250	Relative peace, no fighting, flexibility.
	Courage	200	The first step to personal power.
	Pride	175	Self-importance, even with dependency.
	Anger	150	Fury as an impulse for change.
	Desire	125	Ambition with lack, need.
Basement	Fear	100	Paralysis, anxiety, distrust.
	Grief	75	Deep sadness, limiting nostalgia.
	Apathy	50	Nothing matters, loss of vital impulse.
	Blame	30	Self-punishment, self-sabotage, constant judgment.
	Shame	20	Invisible, unworthy, worthless.

GRATITUDE 3X

A simple and powerful practice to transform your frequency in minutes.

Gratitude is the key that opens any energetic door.

This practice connects you with the power of your story, your present, and your vision.

What is it for? Gratitude is one of the highest frequencies in the universe.

This exercise is designed to help you reconnect with your personal power through conscious appreciation of your past, your present, and your future.

It's a simple yet powerful practice that can shift your frequency in minutes. When you give thanks, you align. When you give thanks, you create space. When you give thanks, you manifest.

~

How to practice it: Think of a difficult situation you've experienced: What did I learn from this? Who am I now because of what I went through? How did it make me stronger? Then write: Thank you for what was. Thank you for what you taught me. Thank you because I survived.

1. **Be grateful for the past**
   - Think of something difficult. Write it down:
     - Thank you for what you taught me. Thank you for making me overcome. Thank you for making me stronger.
2. **Thank you for the present**
   - Recognize what you already have. Write it down:
     - Thank you for who I am. Thank you for what I have today. Thank you for my journey.
3. **Be thankful for the future**
   - Visualize what you desire as if it were already here. Write it down:
     - Thank you for what's coming. Thank you because it's already mine in the quantum field. Thank you for what I will receive.

Integration phrase:

Do this practice every time you feel like you're losing your center. Gratitude brings you back home. Gratitude is not about denying the pain. It's about choosing to see the light within it.

SACA SACA THERAPY DANCE

Release what weighs you down. Receive what lifts you up. Connect and integrate.

Do you feel something stuck in your chest, back, throat, or mind? Do you feel heavy, overwhelmed, stuck, or simply… weighed down?

Sometimes, you don't need to understand it all. You just need to **move it.** Shake it. Release it. And then replace it with intention.

That's how my favorite practice for releasing burdens and making space for light was born: **Saca Saca Therapy Dance.**

~

What is Saca Saca?

- A therapeutic movement.
- A jolt of energy with intention.
- A way to tell your body and soul:
  - *"Take out what no longer belongs to you... and receive what does."*
- A somatic dance.

◎ What does it do?

- Release trapped emotions and stagnant energy.
- Reset your system from the body, not just the mind. Recover your joy, presence, and power.
- Reprogram your frequency by replacing the old with the new.

~

🏃 How is it practiced?

1. Put on some music with a powerful tribal rhythm, drum, Afrobeat, or Latin rhythm. Let it ignite your body without fear of being criticized.
2. Stand tall. Breathe deeply. Close your eyes.
3. Connect with what you want to let go of (anger, anguish, judgment, fear...).
4. Connect with what you want to receive (confidence, peace, joy...).
5. Start shaking! Literally. From head to toe.
6. Say out loud or in your head:
   - I release fear... and receive trust.
   - I release anger... and receive compassion.
   - I release sadness... and receive joy.
   - I release guilt... and receive forgiveness.
7. Repeat strongly. Feel it. Let it out.

8. Move freely, without form, without judgment. Laugh, cry, scream if you need to.
9. When you feel you've released everything, stop.
10. Breathe. Hands on your heart. Say:
    ○ *Thank you, body. Thank you, emotion. Thank you, life.*
11. Receive. Stay for a moment in the lightness.

~

When to use this practice?

- When you're emotionally overwhelmed.
- Before an important meeting or event.
- When closing a cycle or a relationship.
- Every morning to reenergize your energy.
- When you need to return to yourself.

~

Why does it work?

- Because **energy cannot be destroyed—it can only be transformed.**
- Because **your body knows what it needs.**
- Because **movement is medicine.**

~

Final message:

Saca Saca Therapy Dance is not just a practice...

It's a ritual of release and manifestation.

Every time you shake something out of your body, mind, or soul, you make space for something higher.

It's not just about letting go.

It's also about **choosing what you want to receive.**

Shake it all out. Shake it with intention. Welcome the new with love.

Saca saca, baby. You've got this.

QUANTUM MANIFESTATION PROCESS

A vibrational path, not a linear one.

This process flows through four sacred phases, each carrying unique codes of evolution.

It's not a method for asking, but an energetic preparation for **receiving**.

Manifestation is not a straight line. It's a quantum journey, full of expansion and contrast, where your desire, your faith, your frequency… and your ability to hold what you ask for are all tested.

This process has **four sacred phases**, and each one carries its own codes of evolution. It's not a method for asking. It's an energetic **preparation for receiving.**

∾

QUANTUM MANIFESTATION PROCESS

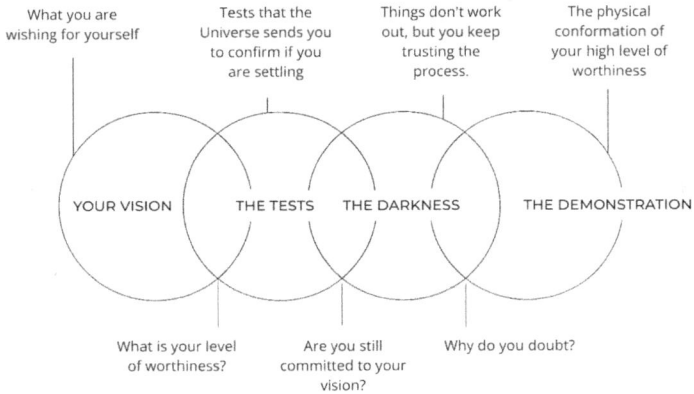

What you are wishing for yourself	Tests that the Universe sends you to confirm if you are settling	Things don't work out, but you keep trusting the process.	The physical conformation of your high level of worthiness

YOUR VISION   THE TESTS   THE DARKNESS   THE DEMONSTRATION

What is your level of worthiness?	Are you still committed to your vision?	Why do you doubt?

1. YOUR VISION

What you're desiring for yourself.

This is where the seed is planted. It's that burning desire that makes you vibrate. A vision that doesn't come from the ego, but from the soul. Something you imagine and, when you think about it... your body shivers, your heart swells with excitement, and your energy rises.

Practice:

- Write in vivid detail what you wish to manifest.
- Close your eyes and imagine you're already living it.
- Breathe and observe: What do you feel? What moves you?
- **Key question:** What is your level of worthiness? Do you feel ready to receive what you're asking for?

Real example:

You want to manifest a house. Visualize yourself in it. Smell the aroma of coffee in your kitchen, hear your children's laughter, feel the peace of having your own space. If something makes you uncomfortable...

that's the wound that still needs healing in order to raise your sense of worthiness.

~

2. THE TESTS

Tests the Universe sends to see if you're settling.

When you make a powerful request, the universe doesn't answer with a "yes" or "no." It says: show me who you are now. That's why tests appear: delays, doubts, obstacles, temptations to go back or settle for less.

Practice:

- Instead of getting frustrated, observe yourself.
- What are you feeling? What is rising to the surface?
- Be grateful for the test. It's an opportunity to choose differently.
- **Key question:** Are you still committed to your vision, even when it seems like it's not working?

Real example:

You've decided to manifest a healthy relationship. And suddenly, your ex shows up. Coincidence? No. It's the universe asking you: Have you truly let go? Are you really done settling for what you had before?

~

3. THE DARKNESS

Nothing seems to be happening, but you keep trusting the process.

This is the most challenging moment. The silence. The "nothing's happening." The feeling of emptiness. This is where many people give up... not knowing they are just about to manifest. This is the quantum space where the soul grows stronger and the ego dissolves.

Practice:

- Take pauses to meditate, pray, or breathe deeply.
- Don't make impulsive decisions.
- Write a letter to the universe saying: "I trust, even if I can't see it."
- **Key question:** Why do you doubt?

Real example:

You're manifesting a career change and suddenly, no one is calling you back. You start to think you made a mistake. But in reality, the silence is integration. The universe is arranging what you asked for. Your job is not to sabotage it.

~

4. THE DEMONSTRATION

The physical confirmation of your high level of worthiness.

And one day… it arrives. You see it. You touch it. You live it. But it's not magic. It's vibrational coherence. It's the result of your energetic, emotional, and spiritual work. You receive what you are able to hold.

Practice:

- Celebrate, give thanks, and honor the process.
- Don't downplay your achievement.
- Notice who you've become.
- Remember: what arrives is a reflection of your inner self.

Real example:

You reach the goal. You step onto the stage. You sign the contract. You walk into your new home. And you feel peace. Not because you "made it," but because you created it.

~

FINAL REFLECTION

Each phase is essential. Don't avoid them. Don't judge them.

Live them with awareness. Hold your energy. Make space.

Manifestation doesn't happen when you're ready on the outside…

It happens when you're ready on the inside.

It's not magic. It's frequency.

~

THANK YOU

THANK YOU

THANK YOU

For reading me and stepping into my life through my story.

Now I'd love to get to know yours and walk alongside you on your transformation journey.

I invite you to follow me on social media, write to me, share your experience, and become part of my community.

With this QR code, you'll get access to:

- Oracle Deck – *The Universe Says*
- Saca Saca Therapy – Song on Spotify
- Sanando Ando Club – WhatsApp Group
- Sanando Ando Podcast – Podcast on Spotify
- Letter to the Universe – Online Manifestation Program
- TEDx Talk – *frequency is the Solution* on YouTube
- Book – *A Kingdom With More Wisdom* on Amazon

See you on the other side,
in the frequency of love, expansion… and the magic you already
are.

www.ingramcontent.com/pod-product-compliance
Lightning Source LLC
LaVergne TN
LVHW052029080426
835513LV00018B/2244